THE HEIRS OF
KING VE

CULTURE & POLITICS
IN ROMAN BRITAIN

THE HEIRS OF KING VERICA

CULTURE & POLITICS IN ROMAN BRITAIN

MARTIN HENIG

TEMPUS

First published 2002

PUBLISHED IN THE UNITED KINGDOM BY:

Tempus Publishing Ltd
The Mill, Brimscombe Port
Stroud, Gloucestershire GL5 2QG
www.tempus-publishing.com

PUBLISHED IN THE UNITED STATES OF AMERICA BY:

Tempus Publishing Inc.
2 Cumberland Street
Charleston, SC 29401
1-888-313-2665
www.arcadiapublishing.com

Tempus books are available in France and Germany
from the following addresses:

Tempus Publishing Group   Tempus Publishing Group
21 Avenue de la République   Gustav-Adolf-Straße 3
37300 Joué-lès-Tours   99084 Erfurt
FRANCE   GERMANY

Copyright © Martin Henig, 2002

British Library Cataloguing in Publication Data.
A catalogue record for this book is available from the British Library.

ISBN 0 7524 1960 9

Typesetting and origination by Tempus Publishing.
PRINTED AND BOUND IN GREAT BRITAIN

Contents

List of illustrations

Text figures

Colour plates

Acknowledgements

This book is dedicated, with love and gratitude, to my brother Stephen who as an imaginative writer has helped me to approach Roman British studies in a new way. We have visited sites together, especially in Gloucestershire and Gwent/Monmouthshire, and have speculated on the ground as to what houses, villas and military barracks were like to live in, before they fell into ruin.

My father introduced me to philosophy at an early age, and my mother to fine art and to literature, especially poetry, thus providing me with life-long interests; in some ways my use of these to underpin this Romano-British odyssey is a tribute to them. I have also been lucky in my archaeological mentors, especially Jocelyn Toynbee, Ralph Merrifield, Graham Webster and my 'archaeological aunt', Zoë Josephs; without their early encouragement, I would not now be writing about the subject. At Oxford (Sir) John Boardman aroused my interest in Greek archaeology and art and Peter Brown opened up new lines of enquiry into Late Antiquity.

I have been stimulated by many innovative and inspirational friends, particularly Tristan Arnison, Richard Bradley, Max Butcher, Marian Campbell, Derek Content, Elizabeth Cook, Audrey Cruse, Graham Davies, Roger Deakin, Elisabeth de Bièvre, Alison and Ken Fincham, Christine Finn, David Ganz, Brian, Lauren and Theowen Gilmour, Lauren Golden, Tamasin Graham, the late Michael Mainwaring, Arthur Macgregor, Helen Molesworth, Margaret Mullett, Beatrice Munby, Julian Munby, John Onians, Isabelle Onians, Nigel Ramsay, Philip Redpath, Gertrud Seidmann, John Steane, Alison Taylor, the late Tania Tinkoff, Percival Turnbull and Simon Watney, all following disparate historical, literary or artistic pursuits, for the most part having little to do with Roman Britain. By keeping me in tune with the diversity of culture, they have prevented me from developing a myopic fixation on too narrow a subject area. There are two specific debts highly relevant to the genesis of this book amongst them. First, by giving me Edgar Wind's *Pagan Mysteries in the Renaissance* almost 40 years ago, John Onians fired my interest in Neo-Platonism which has led me to look beyond the material remains of the past to the transcendence of the spirit which unites us with our forbears. Secondly, a crucial moment of revelation occurred during a tutorial in Oxford a couple of years ago when Helen Molesworth, then my pupil, with her acute scholarship helped me to appreciate the Imperial iconography of the pediment of the temple of Sulis Minerva at Bath, after which so many apparently unrelated observations fell naturally into place.

Amongst scholars mainly concerned with Roman Britain, I am particularly grateful to Catherine Johns, Kenneth Painter and the late Tom Blagg for illuminating discussions about art, architecture and religion in the province. Roger Tomlin and

Mark Hassall have shared their encyclopaedic knowledge of epigraphy, especially the graffiti and cursive documents, which bring us so close to the very thoughts of the Roman Britons. At the two ends of the narrative, John Creighton has reinforced my belief that the story of Roman Britain (and of Romano-British culture) should really begin many years before AD 43, and Charles Thomas and David Howlett, together with Richard Sharpe and Ken Dark, have demonstrated conclusively that it certainly had not ended in 410 or thereabouts. In addition David Sturdy, the author of a fascinating book on King Alfred, has from my first arrival in Oxford been a marvellously unconventional illuminator of by-ways of archaeology. However, my pre-eminent debt is, here, to Grahame Soffe whose polymathic knowledge of the archaeology of Southern Britain, together with practical support (such as the provision of photographs) has been of inestimable value.

Within the region central to this study, there are some more specific acknowledgements. First, in Hampshire, together with Tony King and the late Bob Downey, Grahame Soffe excavated the very important early temple on Hayling Island and worked with me on elucidating the significance of the Thruxton villa. With regard to Oxfordshire, I am of course indebted to Paul Booth, with whom I recently co-authored a volume entitled *Roman Oxfordshire*. Eberhard Sauer has revealed the existence of a vexillation fortress at Alchester on what I believe to be the northern frontier of the early Roman protectorate. Credit for appreciating the significance of Akeman Street as a *limes*, I must share with Roger Ainslie. Jean Bagnall-Smith has written wisely on religious sites in Roman Oxfordshire. Paul Robinson has kept me *au fait* with finds in Wiltshire as has Bryn Walters, excavator of Littlecote; the latter has not only been a fount of knowledge on the northern part of the county, but has given me a number of valuable and refreshingly unorthodox insights into the religion and culture of later Roman Britain in general. In Dorset my informants have included Jo Draper, Laurence Keen and Roger Peers. Latterly Debbie Day, whose thesis on the county I have the privilege of supervising, has been a particular stimulus. For West Sussex, apart from a special debt mentioned below, the late Alec Down was always a reliable, down-to-earth source of information. Finally, Adrian Marsden, a numismatist extraordinaire, has always been enormously helpful in answering my questions on Roman numismatics.

A great debt of thanks is owed, too, to the members of the British Archaeological Association, to the Oxford Wednesday club and the Outside Archaeology group. Election to a Supernumerary Fellowship of Wolfson College, Oxford has been an unexpected privilege, bringing me great conversation and many welcome cups of coffee on the terrace of the common room, where I can contemplate the watery beauties of the Cherwell valley, apparently unchanged for generations.

I feel, more than ever, close to an exciting, new highly creative generation and, unlike Halvard Solness, very much welcome their 'knocking at the door', which is none too soon, beginning to refashion British society and hopefully the environment in which we live for the better, against the twin pressures of materialism and commercialism. This book is very much aimed at them. Alive to the achievements of the past, they will do their best to equal and surpass them, just as I have attempted to show the succeeding generations of Roman and post-Roman Britain building upon their legacy of history and myth. Amongst them several are named above; there are many others, including my godson Edward Gilmour. This book is especially for you!

As a monolingual speaker of English, I have had the temerity to make my characters talk and meditate in my own language, although the patterns of thought in other tongues would certainly have been subtly different in a great many ways. Clearly, until we reach the period of the 'West Saxons' they would naturally have spoken Celtic or Latin, and written almost exclusively in the latter, and the Old English which came in with the Gewissae and was the natal speech of Alfred is scarcely the language we use today. I hope my friends in Gwent, at the University of Wales, Newport, Miranda Aldhouse-Green and Ray Howell, as well as those in other parts of the Principality, notably Anne Ross, will forgive me for this lapse and I trust that, maybe, one day, it can be remedied through translation.

There is one final debt. The archaeologist who has been pre-eminent in revealing so much of the early story of southern Roman Britain, excavating at Fishbourne, Bath and now the villas around Danebury is, of course, Barry Cunliffe. Without his important discoveries (and splendid publications) the book would have been infinitely harder to write and very much the poorer in content. I am privileged to have dug with him at Fishbourne when King Togidubnus' great garden was discovered, feeling my way, trowel in hand, falteringly around the curving bedding trenches, now beautifully replanted with box hedges. I have speculated on the character and achievements of the king ever since and have come to think of him as an old friend. This book is, in part, the result of that empathy.

Some illustrations are my own, others are from the Institute of Archaeology, Oxford, from Philip de Jersey (Celtic Coin Archive, Institute of Archaeology, Oxford) and, of course, Grahame Soffe.

Foreword

In some ways this book may be seen as the sequel to my *Religion in Roman Britain* (1984) and *The Art of Roman Britain* (1995), both published by Batsford for Peter Kemmis Betty. I always intended to produce a third volume on culture and literacy in general, but although at some points this book fulfills that brief, Peter and other readers will not be slow to notice that I have revised my approach radically, not only in presentation but also in content: I now believe that Roman Britain was, in very large part, the indigenous creation of the Britons themselves and it is they, not the soldiers who quickly passed through the settled part of the province on their way to an (often empty) frontier-land, who are the real heroes and heroines of the story; the earlier books placed far too great a stress on the impact of the Roman army and of Roman officialdom.

Here an attempt is made to look at the provincials, more particularly those of the southern part of Britain, in a new way, redefining their roles in relation to Rome and suggesting that from the very beginning until they ceased in any true sense to be 'Romans' they (or at least their élites) controlled their own destinies. If one starts to question the reliability of long-held assumptions, such as the reason for the 'invasion', the reliability of Roman historians such as Tacitus, or the primary importance of the army in Roman Britain, it is like levering blocks of stone out of a wall. Sooner or later the entire edifice totters and comes crashing down. Consequently this book presents what to many will be a radical and unfamiliar view of the subject. Some of my former teachers and those colleagues who have followed in the path of looking at Roman Britain as an essentially military province will inevitably shake their heads and regard it as obtuse.

Culture is central to the understanding of the developments I chronicle. In R.C. Sherriff's moving play for radio, *The Long Sunset* (1955), Roman settlers see the departure of 'The Legions' with misgiving. Sherriff was, of course, examining the end of the British Empire and the fate of expatriots. In this book it is suggested that the army was often the problem and that in fact civilization was often better off without naked military might. In the so-called Dark Ages what collapsed was often what is now called the infrastructure. It appears that what survived, and even flourished, was the Latin language joined, eventually, by several vernaculars. The real Romans of Roman Britain were natives just as in parts of the former British Empire, the English language and British ideas have found a secure home with former subjects of the Raj.

How was I to explain this? I have taken what may seem a novel approach in a book of this sort. In addition to a conventional academic text, I have in places attempted to reanimate the past with living people, some of them known to history: Verica the king, Togidubnus (whom the old books called Cogidubnus, though Togidubnus is the name prefered now by scholars), Aurelius Ambrosianus (Arthur?), St Augustine, King Alfred and Asser for example. Others I have lifted from inscriptions, thus Primus, Catavacus, Bellicia, Lucius Septimius, Avitus, Aurelius Ursicinus and the girl who in the narrative I have made his wayward daughter, the Lady Juliana. Others I have invented, the Greek *grammaticus* Strato for instance, though there were certainly such Greeks in Britain from early on such as Demetrius, perhaps the *grammaticus* Demetrius of Tarsus known to Plutarch, who made a dedication when at York 'to Ocean and Tethys' in the style of Alexander the Great's dedication at the mouth of the river Indus in 325 BC (*RIB* 663). If he was Plutarch's friend, he lived in the first century, more than 150 years before the time I have placed Strato. Strato is altogether wiser; Demetrius was clearly bowled over by Graeco-Roman myth-making about the lands beyond Ocean and the end of the world. The mosaicists Severus and especially his son Candidus represent the originality of the creative artist at the highest level; there certainly were such men and I wish we really did have Candidus' signature on the Stonesfield mosaic: I love him very much. In one way these vignettes should be regarded in much the same way as the artistic impressions freely employed by other writers on Roman Britain, for instance Guy de la Bédoyère, though theirs take the form of reconstruction drawings of buildings in the landscape. My 'reconstructions', by contrast, are verbal, but I hope by and large they too represent a reality which truly existed. But of course within the structure of the book they are there to lead us round the dance of the years, from the violent beginning at the time of Verica's flight (the only 'fall' in the book) to the tranquil close in Asser's study.

As a Platonist, I have deliberately conceived of the entire work as a kind of circular dance in which rebirth and a return from man's fallen state back to one of original perfection are central elements. I have set a dance, which is the occasion both for an erotic encounter between lovers and of communion with the gods, at the very heart of the book, in the middle of chapter 5. The factual reason for this is, of course, to try to explain something of the very intense, spiritual passion which lay behind the great Corinian-school mosaics, perhaps the best art of the Romano-British 'Golden Age', and which seems to work better in such a semi-fictional guise than as a bald description and explanation of, say, the Stonesfield mosaic itself. Very few writers on Roman Britain have been concerned with the living power of the divine, rather than simply dissecting information about religious practices and the gods. In fact Kenneth Grahame's evocation of Pan before Rat and Mole in chapter vii of *The Wind in the Willows* (1908), entitled 'The Piper at the Gates of Dawn', gets closest to representing the mind-changing nature of such an encounter. The Stonesfield episode here represents a similar meeting between the mortal and the immortal for a less puritan and more adult reader, and is likely to be true to the spirit of ecstatic religion in Roman Britain. I hope it has something to say to our own age too. Catavacus and Bellicia, whose names are charmingly inscribed on a pottery pan pipes from Shakenoak, together with their friends Bellicus and Candidus, certainly seem more 'real' to me, more truly Verica's heirs, than many others in this book. They are the antithesis of such flawed monsters as Queen Boudica, the Emperor Constantine or Paulus 'the chain', recorded here, but whose dark cruelties we will never understand. Beyond Roman Britain, outside the realm normally allotted to archaeology, there is a moral, a philosophical and, ultimately, a transcendental story to be told.

Every book needs its heroines or heroes and this book has a number. Amongst the Britons, Togidubnus has to stand pre-eminent, both as Verica's immediate heir and as the man who more than any other seems to me to have shaped the future of his people in a land, part of which came to be known simply as the *Regnum*, 'the Kingdom', and its inhabitants as the *Regni*. Tacitus, alas, merely provides one meagre sentence: 'Certain states were presented to King Togidubnus [or Cogidubnus; the text is corrupt at this point], who maintained his unswerving loyalty down to our own times – an example of the long-established Roman custom of employing even kings to make others slaves.' (Tacitus, *Agricola* 14. trans. H. Mattingly). To this, epigraphy adds the dedication of the temple to Neptune and Minerva at Chichester (*RIB* 91) erected *ex auctoritate Tiberi Claudi [To]gidubni Reg(is) Magni Brit(anniae)*. However, a great deal more can, in my opinion, be deduced, and I find myself a great admirer of the man. His possible relationship with Claudius and Vespasian has seemed worth a little speculation. I would like to have said a bit more about Queen Cartimandua, but she spent her active career too far north. She ditched her dour husband Venutius for his attractive squire Vellocatus: my old friend Mark Hassall imagined a Hollywood-style film with Cartimandua exclaiming as Vellocatus drove his chariot past 'I want that man!' It may have happened; after she lost her lands and had to be rescued by the Romans did she flutter her eyelashes at Togidubnus, or was he too old or too wise? History alas records nothing.

From a later period, the Emperor Carausius is certainly a ruler I can warm to, not least for his sense of style and his ready appeal to culture, to Vergil's great poems, in his propaganda. His reign introduces a theme on which I first became enthusiastic as a student 35 years ago, and on which I wrote a paper, not then published but which has come to fruition here: the tension that seems to have arisen between the provincials and the central government from at least the time of the Carausian revolt and which manifested itself by uprisings on average once a decade. I believe an educated and articulate élite, probably largely a pagan élite with pronounced neo-platonic beliefs, was behind this restlessness.

I have continued the narrative well beyond AD 400, suggesting how something important survived from 'Roman' Britain right through the Dark Ages into the time of the Gewissae and on into the years of the making of the kingdom of Wessex. The story of Wessex continued beyond that, of course, and a fascinating and complex tale it is, yet I intended originally to end with the Augustinian mission, and its aftermath, specifically as far as our region is concerned, with St Birinus and the foundation of the see of Dorchester (*Dorcic*). But I could not resist an epilogue showing Alfred, another 'Great King', and his friend the Welshman, Asser uniting all the strands of what had happened in the previous eight or nine centuries. Both heavyweight intellectuals, it might even have happened like that!

Through all the changes of lifestyle over time there runs a strong thread of continuity made up of overlapping human lives. Thus, we see the tribes of southern Britain becoming incorporated in what was at first a Roman protectorate, then the civilised heartland of the province of Britain (analogous in some respects with the Roman Provincia of *Narbonensis*, Provence in Gaul), then Britannia Prima and ultimately (Anglo-Saxon) *Wessex* as it remains, at least as an intellectual and literary construction, to this day. The frontiers of this zone were ever-changing. Verica's realm at its greatest extent stretched from the south coast to the Thames in West Sussex, eastern Hampshire and Berkshire/south Oxfordshire, though even before AD 40 the northern part of his territory was lost. In effect the events of AD 43 brought the old Atrebatic kingdom, the Dobunni of the Cotswolds and the western Catuvellauni into alliance and with the addition of Belgic lands this comprised Togidubnus's realm. Later the pacified and Romanised Durotriges were brought in, and Britannia Prima probably also comprised south Wales and Dumnonia. There is no evidence as to the frontier separating Britannia Prima from the Consular province of *Maxima Caesariensis*, though I suspect that the latter was quite small, centred around London and its hinterland, perhaps part of the Imperial patrimonium, although southern East Anglia (with Colchester) and also part of Kent may have been included. *Flavia Caesariensis* around York may also have been much smaller than Britannia Secunda, comprising most of north Britain, though powerful administratively and in military affairs. The very late Roman period (after *c*.400) saw further complications. The west of what had been Britannia Prima long remained as a visible region though divided into independent Celtic kingdoms; central-southern Britain was associated with the Gewissae and the Bath-Cirencester region with the *Hwicce* with their Mercian connections. But frontiers were ever in a state of flux and to some degree Alfred restored the territorial integrity of the region to what it had been under the Roman Emperors.

Apart from the land itself, another constant is human nature in its infinite variety. Through this narrative, my own view of the essentially benign spirit in people, despite the inescapable evidence of evil, is very much to the fore. From the time of the first (Claudian) Roman intervention in Britain in 43 to the Augustinian Mission at the end of the sixth century, men and women of goodwill were conscious of the importance of the spiritual and the divine in shaping their lives. We, at the start of the third millennium, could do no better than to follow them.

A most powerful influence in writing this book has been a lifetime love of classicism in art, as expressed in French school painting of the seventeenth century, notably Nicolas Poussin (1593/4-1665) and Claude Gellée (Lorrain) (1600-82). Indeed, I have been haunted by Nicolas Poussin's great painting 'A Dance to the Music of Time' in the Wallace Collection, painted in 1638-40, and I, like Giulio Rospigliosi, Poussin's patron, see the history of which I write as a cosmic dance. The painting at once puts me in mind of the mosaics of the Corinian Orpheus school which I extol in this book and whose structure is likewise a wheel of Fortune, a wheel of life. I find it hard not to see the Classical world through a Claude glass, and in the Ashmolean Museum at Oxford we are lucky to have Claude's late masterpiece painted in Rome in 1682, 'Landscape with Ascanius shooting the Stag of Silvia'. What especially connects such a canvas with my theme is the feeling for the tranquility of the countryside, for landscape fecund with mythology. Claude's paintings virtually rebuilt English sensibilities and we would be wrong to divorce ourselves from the empathy with the past that Claude and his English imitators, such as Richard Wilson (1714-82), have left us. It is clear from the letters of the younger Pliny, for example, that the concept of Poetic Landscape goes back to Antiquity, and what Poussin and Claude do so brilliantly is to present it to us in an instantly accessible manner.

In revealing the world of Britain in the first millennium, a number of compromises have had to be made. First, selection is inevitable, not just in places mentioned or historical incidents discussed but in the sort of people I have chosen to represent: on the whole the educated, more or less well-to-do and above all Romanised section of society. I am sorry if this is 'politically incorrect' but my theme is largely concerned with provincial Roman culture and not those left outside it. Secondly, much more account could be made of language, not just the fact to which allusion was made in the acknowledgements, that Brittonic Celtic would have been the most widespread spoken language with Latin in general use in speech, and the universal medium in writing. There is room for another, much more technical book on what can be learned from surviving writing tablets, curse tablets and graffiti not only about language but thought-patterns. Finally I have given all dates as BC (BCE) or AD (CE). I was tempted to date everything *Ab Urbe Condita* (AUC), that is from 776 BC, the traditional date of Rome's foundation, though that might have seemed rather precious and could certainly have been confusing to modern readers; besides other chronological systems were also in use at the time.

It would be totally impossible to be representative in assembling illustrations in a book of this compass, and those *exempla* I have chosen can, perhaps, best be regarded as a self-contained picture essay, alongside the conventional text and the reconstructed meditations and narratives. The possible list of objects, not to speak of the landscapes (chalk and limestone hills, lush river valleys, fertile farmland, dark forest and the long expanse of the south coast), the weather (temperate with plentiful rainfall), flora and fauna of our area which make it special, is literally endless and no doubt other writers faced by the same body of evidence would come up with a quite different selection.

Introduction

Prologue: The Fall of Troy

'A certain Bericos who had been thrown out of Britain because of political trouble persuaded Claudius to send a force there . . .' (Cassius Dio lx, 19).

16 September, AD 40. Chichester harbour. Dawn.

It was a grey, chilling day; squally gusts of wind blew spray into the face of the old king and his companions, his chamberlain, Saenus, Latin secretary and faithful pilot. The kingdom was undoubtedly lost. One by one each forward line in the great system of dykes had given way, and now revolt had broken out in the oppidum itself. So many, so many of his 'friends' desperately wanted to be on the winning side of Caradoc (whom the Romans called Caratacus) and his brother, Togodumnus. Their father, Cunobelin, who over the years he had come to respect, and even to like, would never have let them do it. But he was now dead and no help could be expected of the crazy Emperor of the Romans.

Gaius had marched his great army up to the sea-shore at Boulogne and declared war on the realm of Neptune, firing great rocks into the foaming Ocean. Worse was to come. In a fit of horrifying infantilism, the Emperor had ordered the soldiers to fill their helmets with sea-shells, starfish and the gods only knew what else and take them back to Rome as war-booty!

Verica thought back to a day, well over half a century ago, when he was taken to the shore, and then rowed across Chichester harbour on a boat to the sacred island of Hayling. There he had played at hillforts making mounds of sand and pebbles . . . and shells. That is what children did, and had always done, no doubt. He imagined the piles of rotting molluscs and decaying seaweed carried on carts through Gaul and down into Italy, past hundreds and thousands of bemused provincials lining the route. Caradoc had heard of this appalling performance within two days. What would he have done if as an ambitious young man he had found an enemy tribe so clearly stripped of its defender? 'Emperor of Rome' – 'Emperor of a children's playground' more like!

Yesterday evening had been unusually clear. He had looked out on the last starlit night of the now shrunken realm of the Atrebates. What did the stars foretell? There had been no comet like that which had portended Julius Caesar's death before he was born, in the days of his father, King Commius. It was strange that Saenus, only an amateur astrologer admittedly, had not been too downhearted. Indeed he saw great prospects; but was Saenus only humouring him, trying to keep his spirits up in impossible times? You did not need the stars to tell you about the kingdom he had lost to the enemy to the north and the jackal Durotriges to the west. Where were its forests now; its lovely rivers, the Arun, the Itchen, full of trout; its gentle downs; its varied coast, chalk cliffs and mud flats, its industrious, intelligent people? What would his beloved father have said? Perhaps he would have reflected, philosophically, that all things decay in due course. And this was the end of the kingdom he had nurtured!

The only ray of hope for him was the little boy, his nephew, whom he had packed off to Rome a few years before. The odd message he had had from him, or from his tutor, since then said he had fared well, and was enjoying himself in the capital of the world. Togidubnus had written in a clear, confident, if still boyish, hand that he had met lots of other princes in the special palace school, the *paedagogium*, at Rome and also one or two real grown up kings, mainly from the East. He especially liked Herod Agrippa from Judaea. Agrippa was a Jew but he showed Togidubnus the temples and attended sacrifices, laughingly saying 'When in Rome . . .'. He had told him that some kings in his part of the world had traditionally used swanky titles, 'King of Kings', 'Great King' and other such phrases, and that he had an ambition to become even more famous than his grandfather, Herod 'the Great'. That Herod may have been a friend of Rome but, by all accounts, he was a peculiarly nasty piece of work with a penchant for massacring his own citizens; Agrippa was quite different, genuinely humane and thoughtful. It was he who had introduced Togidubnus to a nice old man in the palace library, some sort of relative of Caesar who knew the Celtic tongue and spoke it like a native; this Claudius had also been very good to him too and taught him to speak Greek as well as Latin . . . and thrown in a bit of Etruscan for luck! Maybe Togidubnus, with the help of his new friends, could make his own last days comfortable at Baiae or Pompeii, somewhere by the sea, somewhere by the sea . . .

Verica was recalled from his reverie by the anxious pilot. The contrary wind had now dropped. It was not safe to stay at anchor a moment longer. The royal compound had been fired by the insurgents . . . you could see the flames, a hideous red glow to the north . . . they would be looking for him now! He tried not to think what must be happening to the women. Saenus gave the order. The little vessel prepared to cast off from its moorings, the rowers pulled hard on the oars and the ship sped down the creek out into the open waters of the Solent and was soon lost to sight in the enveloping autumnal mists.

In order to make sense of intellectual and social developments during the first five or six centuries of our era, it is necessary to review what we are told by Roman and Greek literary sources, and sometimes to criticise them very drastically indeed. Most histories of Roman Britain use the writings of authorities such as Dio Cassius or Tacitus as though they preserve a more or less factual account of events. While they do, of course, provide some contemporary details about Britain, their obligations were mainly to their Roman audiences who expected to hear traditional-sounding accounts of exploits of generals and armies. Battles were composed of conventional *topoi*, both in their settings and their events. Britain, like other 'military' provinces, was largely a stage-set for heroic exploits, and it is these that form the basis of traditional narratives. Archaeology has frequently been used to supplement and confirm the ancient historians. After all forts and fortresses from Inchtuthil in Scotland to Portchester on the south coast really exist, and have been excavated, so surely they confirm such episodes as the battle of Mons Graupius or the command-structure of the Saxon Shore? The answer to this question is that monuments cannot be translated into historical episodes: they simply give us evidence for the presence of men, in these cases soldiers, and provide pointers to political and military action. The task of the historian is to use all available sources and provide a plausible reconstruction to take account of these, hoping that the result is more than fiction. In doing so the writer must always be aware of other possibilities. In his detailed analysis of first-century literary sources David Braund, in his book *Ruling Roman Britain* (1996), comes to similar conclusions to me in some instances but to very different ones in others. That is inevitable given the scanty and ambiguous nature of the evidence.

To begin at the beginning, the key question which we need to ask ourselves is who were the beneficiaries, both short-term and long-term, of the events of AD 43? Who were the people whose lavish lifestyles are reflected in Roman town houses, country villas with their gardens, mosaics, wall-paintings and gold jewellery? Who feasted in the triclinia or lazed in the baths? The answers to these questions are crucially important. Tacitus amidst his formal *topoi* of *Agricola* 21, answered that the Britons enslaved themselves by adopting a luxurious lifestyle! The quality of this 'slavery' has been brought home to me, visiting the remains of the mighty first-century palace at Fishbourne, or the many fourth-century villas, Bignor, Brading and Littlecote for example, whose mythological mosaics proclaim the culture (*paedeia*) of their proprietors. The great temple of Sulis in Bath, the Cirencester Jupiter column capital, the forum inscriptions of Verulamium and Wroxeter, and the city walls of Silchester and Caerwent have one factor in common. As we will see all were concerned with local power. There could be no greater contrast than that between Norman England after 1066, with its network of intrusive castles dominating the countryside, and the largely peaceful continuity of so much of Roman Britain after AD 43.

It is unfortunate that, apart from a few inscriptions and graffiti, the people of Roman Britain are largely silent for us until one or two ecclesiastical writers at the end of our story, Patrick and Gildas, give them a voice. Across the channel in Gaul the poems of Ausonius and the letters of Sidonius Apollinaris, to take but two, cast a vivid light on a very similar Celtic people living virtually identical lives. Here I have tried to let the Britons speak, placing them in the context of their rich and beautiful landscape, their noble arts and varied religious cults. Archaeological discoveries, properly understood, provides some startling evidence.

Before commencing this study I worked with Dr Paul Booth on a study of Roman Oxfordshire, effectively a transect through south-central Roman Britain, and in doing so I increasingly felt that I was exploring a territory totally different from the one I expected to find. It was certainly different from the one I had encountered

1a   *Gold staters. On the left of Verica showing a vine leaf and a horse, and on the right of*
Dubnovellaunus with a patterned obverse and horse and branch reverse.
Institute of Archaeology, Oxford

in almost all the other books about Roman Britain. On the base of a pewter plate
from Appleford was the name of the owner; she was called Pacata. Her parentage is
not recorded, and everything about her is unknown apart from a possible relationship with a man called Lovernianus who also inscribed the plate. However, to own
a piece of pewter she must have had a certain consequence in society; she was not a
slave, nor a peasant and, furthermore, the graffito shows she was literate; the letters
are beautifully executed so she was surely, to some degree, educated. She was
assuredly one of the 'heirs' of the Atrebatan king with whom this book begins.

Verica is only known to us from one reference in Dio and from his varied and
highly sophisticated Roman-style coinage. He was surely a fascinating character.
Interested in more than the superficialities of Roman culture like his contemporaries,
notably Cunobelin, he nevertheless would have remained in Roman eyes a
'barbarian'. Very different was his successor, most probably a close relative: Verica's
immediate heir, Togidubnus (Cogidubnus) struck no coins but from Tacitus, and the
one inscription which mentions him, we know he was a king at least in the

1b Silver minim of Verica depicting a sphinx on the obverse and a hunting dog on the reverse. Institute of Archaeology, Oxford

Chichester region, where the North Street inscription (*RIB* 91) shows he was made a Roman citizen by Claudius. The marble head found at Fishbourne is a private portrait of a boy of about thirteen, the age at which a citizen would assume the *toga virilis*. Such a head must have been carved in Rome or at least in southern Europe, for Britain always lay beyond the marble-carving part of the Empire. I believe this might have been a portrait of the owner of the palace carved when he was a boy in Rome and if so it is very probably a head of Togidubnus, done at the very time Claudius had him made a citizen and gave him his *praenomen* and *nomen*. Later, Tacitus notes his steadfast loyalty to Rome which was rewarded as the inscription records with the title of Great King. The ramifications of the title and the means by which I believe he secured it are the subject of the first part of this book of which he is very properly the hero. Here it is sufficient to note that in the history of these islands the epithet 'Great' has been sparingly given. Indeed, the only other king called great reigned 800 years later, largely over the same land now generally called Wessex. King Alfred and Togidubnus seem to me to have had much in common. For both, warfare was a means to an end, defensive not aggressive, and both were deeply committed to the cultural development of their subjects.

The book will let us wander over much of Britain, but at its core are the lands of central southern Britain and the territories of the Dobunni and Durotriges to the west. In the Roman period what had been Togidubnus' kingdom became in the third century part of Britannia Superior and in the fourth century it very largely corresponded to Britannia Prima which, to judge from its villas and mosaics, was by far the most artistically advanced area of Roman Britain. Major cultural changes in the fifth and sixth centuries saw a reversion to a rather simpler, tribal society, and the core of Britannia Prima became, in large part, the land of the Gewissae, probably of mixed Celtic and Germanic stock, though eventually taking on an 'Anglo-Saxon' identity as the West Saxons. Here our book will end, but it is an intriguing thought that, however remotely, King Alfred was the ultimate heir to Verica and Togidubnus. Or was his reign the last chapter in the story? The line of descent runs on and on, to our own day and I hope, for many generations ahead. This is our legacy!

King Verica comforted his great hound Cunorix who had been the model, he liked to think, of the hound on one of his most attractive coins. The Romans admired British hunting dogs and perhaps he could breed from Cunorix. He was glad that he had managed to stow a chest of bullion for presents to Caesar and offerings to the gods of Rome. He would not think too far ahead.

It was now almost evening but the coast of Gaul was at last in sight, Gesoriacum with the welcoming beacon of its *pharos*. Here was the very place where Gaius Caesar had 'conquered' Neptune and received the submission of Cunobelin's son, Verica's foster-child, Adminius. The lighthouse was at least a material achievement from that ill-fated campaign and a promise of refuge for him and his companions from the storms, not only of the sea but of life itself. Verica determined to follow the example of Adminius and at once submit himself to the authority of Rome in the person of the local commander of the fleet, and request from him an escort to the City, as befitted his rank. The rest was up to Fortune!

1 Verica's kingdom

June AD 35. Chichester harbour.

The ship lay beached in the mud of the creek. It had off-loaded its cargo of amphorae containing fish-sauces, olive-oil and wine, and a few crates of ceramic and bronze table ware; together with some more expensive presents for the king, a cloak shot with gold thread, a silver drinking-service and scrolls containing Vergil's great epic, the *Aeneid*. In addition there was a subvention in cash to help the king to hold together his powerful sub-kings in his alliance with Rome. The passengers on the ship had included a commissioner from the emperor, and Greek and Latin tutors for the king's six-year-old nephew, Togidubnus. These would accompany him on the journey to Boulogne and then through Gaul to Italy where he would be educated and, in his turn, be trained to become king of the Atrebates. The emperor himself, through his ministers, would be responsible for his well-being and in return he would become the emperor's client. Such an arrangement of obligation between men, a network of inter-dependency, held the empire together. Even Caesar was the client of one greater than himself, Jupiter Optimus Maximus.

Beyond Fishbourne creek and scattered so widely over the south Sussex plain that it could scarcely be called a town lay the oppidum. To the outsider all buildings were the same, all were circular huts some larger than others. The small ones were indeed houses; the larger were the dwellings of important tribesmen or even temples of the gods. Across the water lay Hayling Island where a large circular building within a square enclosure was the temple of the war god and his female consort. Here offerings of chariots, swords and shields, and coins from throughout Gaul as well as Roman coins were deposited by numerous votaries anxious to obtain the goodwill of the ancestors buried here; notable was King Commius, one-time friend of Julius Caesar, who, implicated in Vercingetorix's revolt, had fled to Britain, not without adopting a ruse for his ship firmly beached on a sandbank, and the king had to hoist sail to fool his Roman pursuers that he had indeed escaped. Here too lay Commius' successor Tincomarus who had re-established friendship with Rome and was one of those who, as Strabo informs us, by making offerings to Jupiter on the Capitol, had virtually made his kingdom a Roman province.

The ceremony at Verica's hut was short but dignified. The King in a simple plaid garment and a heavy gold torque around his neck, the symbol of his authority, addressed the young Equestrian officer through his confidential Latin secretary, Saenus. He confirmed his friendship to Caesar, the commercial rights of merchants (most of them, of course, Gauls) in his territories, and in return for his cloak and other presents gave Caesar a load of tin ingots, bales of seal-skins and bear-skins, two enormous mastiffs and four Trinovantian slaves, captured in a raid, a rare success against his ever more menacing northern neighbours. After complimenting Caesar he reminded him that the northern part of his realm centred on Calleva was effectively lost to him. In praising the emperor for his past heroism, he hinted that Roman intervention against Eppillus of Calleva would be welcome. He finished by proclaiming that all his hopes lay in Togidubnus, the lively little boy who was playing at his feet, and resisting the best efforts of his nurses to bring him to order.

May AD 39. Rome.

Prince Togidubnus, now dressed in a Greek tunic, sat on the steps of the Paedagogium in Rome. A bright 10-year-old, he spoke both Greek and Latin and had established the trust of other foreign princes, heirs of the remaining Hellenistic dynasties, Great Kings of the East, whose cultures had influenced the Romans so much for centuries. Amongst them were young men like Polemo II of Pontus and the Jewish King, Herod Agrippa, nephew of that Herod the Great, who while certainly the friend of Augustus was a tyrant to his own family (it was said it was better to be Herod's pig than his son) and to his people.

The prince was developing into an excellent student, and the proudest day of his life was when he was given access to the palace library. The new emperor, vain and unbalanced, rather despised learning and it was hardly fashionable to read ancient works of scholarship. The only member of the Imperial family to be seen here was certainly not courted by those who sought influence, though he was a kindly fellow, getting on for middle age, with a great interest in the people of the Empire. He had taught himself Punic and still knew Etruscan and was writing books on Carthaginian and Etruscan history and customs. He quickly befriended the young Briton whom he startled by addressing in faultless Celtic. Claudius reminded him that despite appearances, he was regarded by some as a Gaul himself. After all he had been born in Lyons and spent much of his childhood there. He admitted that he liked and trusted provincial Gauls more than many of the noble-born sycophants of Rome who laughed at him for his lameness and his stutter. To Claudius, Togidubnus revealed his worries about his homeland, the declining health of his ageing uncle, rumours of plots and dissension, and the growing power of the sons of King Cunobelin. Cunobelin himself was a friend of Rome's but his hold on events was slipping. His realm, long a loose confederacy, was falling under the control of others.

The character of Celtic Britain as given by Classical authors and supported to some extent by archaeology is familiar. Although the bulk of the populace consisted of simple farmers, the ruling class consisted of warriors who sometimes fought naked in battle apart from their blue-woad war paint and the flashing gold torques of which fine examples have been found at Snettisham in Norfolk and Ipswich in Suffolk. The warrior carried a long

2 *The Marlborough bucket,*
   in Devizes museum;
   detail with two masks.
   Photo: Grahame Soffe

iron sword which, when not in use, was lodged in a splendid decorated sheath, like the examples from Little Wittenham and Standlake in Oxfordshire. There were long shields sometimes ornamented in enamel like the Battersea shield and helmets of striking design, like the two-horned helmet from Waterloo.

When not fighting life centred around the feast. Great buckets like those from Marlborough, Wiltshire and Aylesford, Kent contained mead, beer or imported wine, providing the mainstay of long drinking bouts. Food consisted of hunks of meat boiled or roasted on spits.

Although women might on occasion fight they were generally seen engaged in domestic occupations like weaving. An upper class woman might own a neck torque and a few items of jewellery such as brooches but her most prized possession was likely to be a mirror with a back engraved in an abstract, curvilinear La Tène style, like the example excavated from a woman's grave at Birdlip in Gloucestershire.

Religion was dominated by the Druidic caste of priests, secret and sinister in reputation, presiding over sacrifices of men as well as animals. Drowning, strangulation and

3 *Decoration on top of scabbard
of sword from Standlake,
Oxfordshire.* Photo: Institute
of Archaeology, Oxford

the cutting of the throat are all known. Sometimes heads were impaled on spikes and
kept separately as trophies. For the druids the mistletoe was sacred, especially when
grown on an oak, as were certain standing stones.

Sanctuaries were natural places, groves called nemets, rivers, lakes and bogs. A
century or so before the events of this book we find structures serving as temples in
such hillfort sites as Danebury in Hampshire and on the sacred island of Hayling
across Chichester harbour, in the same county.

The impression is of a primitive, barbarian society, but as soon as it began to be
recorded by Roman writers, it was no longer that at all. It was in a state of rapid
change. The rulers of the warbands come out of the shadows at least partially; they
inscribe their coins with their names and title in Latin, and maintain diplomatic
relations with the Graeco-Roman world to the south. Many of the rulers might well
have felt distinctly uneasy with their own ancestral rites. Some of them, certainly
Cunobelin and Verica, tried hard to present themselves as civilised allies of Rome.

Originally Cunobelin had ruled from Verlamion, an oppidum of the
Catuvellauni. Dio tells us (60, 20.1-2) that his sons Caratacus and Togodumnus were
Catuvellauni, so presumably Cunobelin was of that tribe too. However, as legends
on coins testify, Cunobelin shifted his capital to Camulodunum, the chief centre of
the Trinovantes. Verica, his contemporary, the successor of Commius who calls
himself 'son of Commius', ruled in the Chichester region; the oppidum probably
occupies an extensive swathe of land marked out by the Chichester Entrenchments.
Verlamion, Camulodunum, the Chichester-Selsey oppidum and Calleva imported

4   *The Battersea shield, length c.75cm.*
    Photo: British Museum

Roman wine, bronzes and other luxury goods through middlemen, *negotiatores*, and developed some of the characteristics of true towns. In his account of Britain the Greek geographer Strabo was able to record that some of the British dynasts had sent embassies to Caesar Augustus and set up dedications on the Capitol (Strabo 4.5). This implies diplomatic activity and the employment of at least literate secretaries.

Literacy will be a major theme of this book and it is important to establish that it had its beginnings in Britain, perhaps as much as a century before the conquest. Evidence includes the legends on coins themselves: the name of a ruler such as Commius, Tincomarus, Tasciovanus or Cunobelin; an affiliation, someone was the son of someone else; or in the case of Verlamion, Camulodunum and Calleva, an issuing centre. Other evidence includes the devices on certain coins which were certainly adapted from seals or gems set in signet rings because they occur nowhere on the Roman coinage, devices like the seated Apollo playing the lyre on a coin of Cunobelin, and the Augustan signet ring containing a gem depicting a maenad from a coin hoard ending with issues of Tincomarus at Alton, Hampshire. In view of extensive Roman imports found, for example, in graves at Welwyn, Hertfordshire and Camulodunum, Essex, Cunobelin was surely one of those friendly kings as were the Atrebatic rulers such as Tincomarus and, later, Verica.

5 *The mirror from a woman's grave at Birdlip, Gloucestershire.* Photo: Courtesy of the late Ralph Merrifield

Coins in general assumed an increasingly Roman appearance both north and south of the Thames. The motifs seem to have been chosen with care and it is possible to read from devices as lions and sphinxes, and deities such as Neptune, Apollo and Victory, a Royal propaganda concerned with power and prosperity, analogous to (and modelled on) the propaganda of Augustus and his successors as displayed on the Imperial coinage. The most famous device on Cunobelin's issues is to be seen on his gold staters, an ear of emmer, a reminder that corn was wealth. Some of Verica's staters show the vine leaf, and symbolise viticulture.

Connexions with the Classical World are shown by imports of wine amphorae, pottery, Campanian bronze vessels and even silver cups. The majority of these finds come from burials in the Catuvellaunian area, notably the rich burials from Welwyn, and the Lexden tumulus in Trinovantian Colchester with Roman bronzes of a boar and a griffin and a silver pendant with a portrait of Augustus. There have also been significant finds from Kent, for instance from Aylesford. However, similar material clearly reached central-southern Britain. The Augustan period gold ring mentioned above and also a typically Roman bracelet found with it in the Alton hoard come into the same category. In some ways even more significant is another gold hoard from near Winchester. This consisted of two chain-linked pairs of gold La Téne brooches and a pair of torques, but unlike the usual torques these were made by weaving together rings of fine gold wire to create flexible ropes, a Mediterranean technique. The brooch chains were made in the same way. The high purity of the gold is also a feature of Graeco-Roman jewellery.

Nevertheless the apparent Romanisation of native culture in southern and south-eastern Britain did not mean that the political situation was stable. Each tribe was composed of a confederacy of different sub-groups often at war one with another. In the days of Caesar's invasion the Romans had intervened to put a certain Mandubracius back on the Trinovantian throne. Such alliances did not, as is sometimes stated, make the Trinovantes as such 'pro Roman'; they only show that one faction at one particular time and for its own purposes sought Roman aid against Cassivellaunus, whose tribal affiliations are, in any case, totally unknown. Tribes tended to fragment, and rulers seem to have moved their power bases from one place to another. The situation, indeed, had something in common with the Balkans today; something in common with the *condottieri* states of Renaissance Italy. Without historical records the chances of understanding what was going on in any detail are virtually non existent.

Cunobelin may, conceivably, have become more hostile to Rome at the end of his reign under pressure from his sons and successors, as is sometimes stated, but this is not really reflected in the coinage and imports. Roman policy was surely to maintain the balance of power in southern Britain and keep the dynasts on good terms with Rome if not with each other. When the Atrebatan ruler Tincomarus was driven out of his realm about AD 7, Augustus gave him succour and seems to have accepted the situation. The northern part of the Atrebatan realm with its capital at Calleva was ruled at this time by another member of the dynasty, Eppillus, who styled himself as *Rex Calle(vae)*. This Eppillus seems also to have ruled in Kent, which he may have taken aggressively, possibly driving out the local king Dubnovellaunus who also sought sanctuary with Augustus. Epillus' expanded realm did not last long and he was replaced at Calleva by Epaticcus of Cunobelin's dynasty. It is possible that Rome even connived at this. Calleva remained in the hands of members of Cunobelin's dynasty for 30 years and it is probable that Caratacus struck his coins here immediately before the Roman intervention.

When, at the end of Cunobelin's reign, his philo-Roman son, Adminius, was driven out of Britain, to surrender himself to Gaius Caligula and seek sanctuary within the Roman Empire, it might appear that the situation was very different from that of 30 years before when Tincomarus was expelled from the southern kingdom. What had changed was that Cunobelin's other sons, Caratacus and Togodumnus, were bent on continuing an aggressive policy and building up a unified realm in the south-east.

The news that Claudius might have received, like any other Roman with an interest in Gaul and Britain, perhaps from the child Togidubnus, was that the confederacy of the Trinovantes and that part of the Catuvellauni associated with it was suborning even the remaining parts of Verica's realm, as well as casting greedy eyes even further afield, on the Dobunni of present day Gloucestershire and west Oxfordshire. Claudius could only nod thoughtfully, realising that the situation in

6   *Two Roman images on coins of Cunobelin: a Apollo, from a Hellenistic group showing the god looking on while the satyr, Marsyas is flayed; b a lion-griffin.*
Institute of Archaeology, Oxford

Britain was a potential threat to the security of the neighbouring parts of Gaul. What neither he nor Togidubnus would have dared to voice was that there was precious little help Rome could give while its ruler was a maniac.

The fiasco AD 40; Boulogne

Gaius was conscious of being heir to Julius Caesar whose name (C. Iulius Caesar) he bore. Campaigning against the Germans and over the sea in Britain could be seen as fulfilling Caesar's work. Unfortunately it seems that the externals of victory over Ocean were all that really mattered to Gaius. He assembled troops at Boulogne, confronting Ocean with his artillery, and had his soldiers collect sea shells as spoils. The one tangible result of this campaign was his lighthouse, while his control over the exile Adminius proved his power over the rulers of Britain.

It is certain that some account of this attempt to represent a symbolic victory would have got back to Britain where its niceties would certainly not have been understood. While Rome's receiving of an exile would not have had much impact, irresolute and irrational action by the Emperor can only have encouraged Caratacus and his brother into believing they had a free hand in Britain which, in the short term, they did. Gaius's lunacy was but one factor leading to his assassination, and the circumstances of Claudius' accession were not such that immediate action could be undertaken.

During 41, the situation in the southern Atrebatan realm evidently became critical. In the faction-ridden politics of the British tribes the Catuvellaunian rulers and their Atrebatan allies overthrew the Commian dynasty. Verica will have fled to Claudius by now at latest. As he set sail, comforted no doubt that he would meet his Rome-educated kinsman within a few weeks, he must have wondered whether he could hope for more than a small pension, like Tincomarus or Adminius before him.

7   *A Romanising figure of a stag, cast in bronze and found near Brighton, Sussex. Does it date before or after the Roman intervention?* Photo: Christies

In fact by the time he arrived in Rome the situation had changed decisively. There was a new emperor, interested in Gaul and in the Celtic peoples. He also needed a quick victory but it had to be a victory in a place where he could not be accused of irresponsible expansionism. There was also, I suggest, a personal chemistry between the Britons, Togidubnus and Verica, and Claudius, which would fashion future events to the mutual advantage of Romans and Britons. Claudius could restore the Atrebatan client kingdom, which he might have been persuaded he was almost bound to do, however laxly his predecessors had taken their obligation. A client king is not the same as a puppet king; he is a ruler in client relationship to the emperor. There are obligations on both sides. To his British clients it would be as simple as this. Of course, in Rome and further away it could be presented as conquest, or the fulfillment of the Caesarian legacy, and it would enable Claudius to be a true '*imperator*'; perhaps the denouement of himself riding into Camulodunum on the back of an elephant was already in his mind.

Rome, the Imperial Palace. 17 July AD 42.

It was the hottest night of the year. The emperor enjoyed his dinner (a large turbot smothered in mushrooms) as much as usual. But clearly there was serious business to be transacted. No entertainments were in prospect after the meal. The guests included Aulus Plautius, a most distinguished general of Consular rank, one or two other soldiers including a youngish, bluff Sabine, Vespasian, about to be appointed legate of II Augusta, and two Britons, an old man and a boy. Verica wore a blue mantle and a neck-torque as befitted a Celtic king; Togidubnus was much more simply clad in a boy's toga of Roman style. The room was closely guarded. The strategy needed to be decided on. The old man told Claudius he knew the waters of the Solent, and the pilot, his friend Saenus, who had fled with him knew them better. The assault would take the enemy by surprise, at night or at dawn . . . and in winter or early spring. The mistakes made by Caesar, the stoney beach, Commius's detention by hostile tribesmen in 55 BC, would not be repeated.

Claudius asked young Togidubnus what he thought. Togidubnus, fired by his reading, spoke of the wars of Troy, of Alexander and of Scipio. Claudius was delighted by the polished phrasing of his protegé, which would indeed have been unusually fluent even for a true-born Roman. He had always liked Gauls above all other nations, anyway. So he took the opportunity of this feast to announce that nurtured in our culture as he was, he would bestow citizenship and the toga virilis on the lad, hence-forth to be known by his own names, Tiberius Claudius. There was warm applause from all; Claudius embraced him, and Vespasian gave him a firm, friendly handshake. The great adventure was about to begin. The kingdom of the Atrebates would arise again, more splendid than before.

2 The King returns, AD 43

A day in March, AD 43. Boulogne.

The weather was still bitterly cold. The winter had seen driving snow and a persistent, cutting wind from the north. At Boulogne a vast armada of war-galleys and barges for transport was assembled late in the previous year. The Saturnalia had been a welcome few days of light relief, a time of riotous festivity. Soldiers who remembered the unappealing antics of Gaius in the same place a mere three years earlier, guyed the episode, and consumed a mountain of 'booty' consisting of clams, oysters and lobsters. The high spot was a pretend revolt 'put down' by Narcissus, the emperor's confidential freedman secretary, whose appearance on the rostrum was greeted by the traditional cries of '*Io Saturnalia!*' His speech had been humorous and had ended with the offer of three cups of wine to each man as a 'donative', an offer accepted with acclamation . . .

There followed an anxious January and February as troops of the II Augusta, XX Valeria, XIV Gemina, and IX Hispana and many auxiliaries drilled and waited in a vast tented town. To Togidubnus the scenes resembled the Grecian camp before Troy, which were vivid to him from his reading; he sought out his friends, especially old Vespasian who always had a cheerful word for him even when he was busy. Verica tried to drill his own men, a pitifully small group of exiles, in the Roman style. March arrived and after two blustery weeks the wind swung around to the east. It was what everyone had been waiting for. On the 22nd, the entire flotilla was prepared to sail . . . before the campaigning season had properly arrived. Nobody would be expecting them yet. The boats, hundreds of them, cleared the harbour in three divisions and set a course due west.

The night was dark at first but soon there were a few stars. One seemed to shoot across the sky in front of them, along the very direction of their course. Just before dawn, as the sky grew lighter, Togidubnus and Verica, standing in the poop of the lead galley, the *Commius Rex*, saw the peninsular of Selsey to the starboard. There was no sign of activity on the land; the shores were quite deserted. Nobody in Britain knew what was about to happen . . . Verica turned to Saenus. His trusty pilot's knowledge of the local seas, reefs and sand bars came into its own now. Saenus waited a moment and then nodded. The king raised his arms in supplication to the gods of his ancestors. Then, at the signal arranged with the rest of the ships in the flotilla, he dropped them again. Silently all the vessels turned abruptly through 90 degrees and the mariners rowed them hard north towards the still mist-shrouded land. That same creek which had seen Togidubus set off eight years ago to receive a Roman education and a mere couple of years ago had been the scene of Verica's ignominious flight was about to witness the exiles' triumphant return. As the Commius came to rest in the silt at the head of the creek the sun came out, still low in the Eastern sky, its beams flashing on Verica's torque of red gold; he was helped ashore and at once bent down and held a handful of Atrebatic earth aloft. Beside him stood Togidubnus, tall and handsome, wearing a Roman military dress with gilded breastplate and a cloak of red shot through with gold to mark his status as royal heir but no jewellery at all, apart from a discrete gold signet-ring as befitted his rank. The young prince unsheathed his *gladius* from a scabbard richly ornamented in repoussé with acanthus foliage, and portraying Romulus and Remus being suckled by the she-wolf, and raising it in the air led the great shout of 'Victory!' which was taken up by unit after unit from the ships which had arrived already or were within earshot. Others were striking landfall further round the harbour. A flock of small birds crossed the sky and flew inland. The augur nodded: it was a propitious moment for a kingdom reborn.

The great invasion

Does an invasion need to be hostile to the inhabitants of a country being invaded? Modern experience of United Nations actions, for example, should tell us that such action can have an altruistic aim. The popular view of the Roman 'invasion' of AD 43 was that Italians took over and subdued the land of Britain for motives of profit and Empire. However, the reasons were far more mixed as a glance at the composition of the legions and accompanying auxiliaries will show. No doubt there were, indeed, quite a number of Romans of Italian stock including of course the commanders, such as Plautius and Vespasian, but many of the men in the Roman legions were Spaniards and Gauls. There may, already, have been a few Britons. The accusations of enemies are often more truthful than those of friends and in his satire written after Claudius' death in AD 54, Seneca accused the dead emperor of 'wanting to see all the Gauls, Spaniards and Britons in togas' (*Apocolocyntosis* 3, 3). In this case the *casus belli* had been Verica's expulsion. There is no reason to believe that Claudius did not honour his obligations to his client. I have always assumed that Verica lived long enough to be brought back to Britain to finish his reign, though his heir, Togidubnus, whether he was present in 43 or not, no doubt took over before long. His eventful reign provided a change of direction, for he was a different sort of person from his predecessor; he saw himself as a Roman as well as a Briton, a beneficiary of Claudius' friendship and generosity. It must have been inescapable to him that, like Aeneas driven out of Old Troy to found a New Troy, his destiny was likewise to save and nurture his beloved people.

There are many books, probably far too many books, about the military achievements of the Romans. This is not one of them, and it is largely about other aspects of the province, though warfare needs to be mentioned from time to time. Briefly, what seems to have happened first of all was that the oppidum in the Chichester area

8 *Nicolo intaglio from Verulamium depicting an eagle on a war galley, length 14mm.*
Photo: Institute of Archaeology, Oxford

was liberated. The Roman army set up a base camp here, with important facilities on Chichester Harbour, notably at Dell Quay and Fishbourne. It is quite likely that another section of the fleet landed at Richborough (*Rutupiae*) in East Kent at the mouth of the River Wantsum, in order to establish a bridgehead here. There is certainly a Claudian supply base at Richborough and much later the four-way arch (*quadrifrons*) erected here, probably by Domitian, marked Richborough as the point of entry from the continent (the *accessus Britanniae*) if not the official point from which the 'invasion' commenced. A hoard of 34 gold coins dating down to AD 42 from Bredgar near Sittingbourne has been used as evidence for a Kent landing or even as support for a putative 'Battle of the Medway' nearby, but solid evidence is slight. To use Dio's *topos*-rich text to establish a geography of invasion is hazardous and, in any case, I do not believe the major landing could have been in Kent. In the first place the key objective was the liberation of Verica's kingdom, allowing for a swift advance through friendly territory up to the Thames and beyond, to Alchester for example. Second, the Solent area – the '*Magnus Portus*' or in the Middle Ages 'Southampton' – was of key strategic value and the only natural harbour of this sort

9 Sard intaglio from Verulamium showing Diomedes seizing the Palladium, length 13mm.
Photo: Institute of Archaeology, Oxford

on the south coast. Third we have to explain the fact that Vespasian is to be found campaigning in the island of *Vectis* (the Isle of Wight) before moving north against the Durotriges. To judge from the local Iron Age coinage, the ruling dynasty of *Vectis* had been closely connected by ties of blood and culture with the Atrebates, but it was evidently now ruled by vassals of the hated Durotriges, who had taken over the western part of Atrebatic territory. Just as for the ancient Athenians the island of Aegina had been the 'eyesore of the Piraeus'; it was not possible for either the Atrebates or the Romans to be tranquil in mind with this enemy base across the water. Thus, Vespasian moved swiftly with his Second Legion to clear the island of the enemy (Suetonius, *Divus Vespasianus* IV, 1). It was clear that he would have to fight a major campaign on the west side of southern Britain through what is now Dorset, and in the end he is said to have fought 30 battles and taken 20 hillforts before the Durotriges and another tribe (the Dumnonii of Devon perhaps or part of the Dobunni) were subdued. In the east the sons of Cunobelin were the main focus of attack, and the other legions with their commanders and Aulus Plautius were largely responsible for this theatre of war.

Fortunately the Dobunni, or at least a large proportion of that tribe, and the Western Catuvellauni allied themselves firmly with the Atrebates and the Romans. This had the result that the Roman armies were able to make rapid progress through much of central southern Britain without having to garrison these lands very seriously, if at all. No more than establishing essential communication points was necessary. The areas comprising modern Hampshire (various small tribes administratively linked together as the *Belgae*),

*10   Glass intaglio from Alchester
      showing the head of a horse
      within a border made up of a
      curved military trumpet or
      cornu. Photo: Institute of
      Archaeology, Oxford*

Sussex, Berkshire, south Oxfordshire (*Atrebates*), Gloucestershire, west Oxfordshire (*Dobunni*) and central Oxfordshire, south Buckinghamshire and south Hertfordshire (Western *Catuvellauni*) were effectively absorbed into the Empire, and most of this vast territory, the prosperous heartland of Britain, was eventually to be in Togidubnus' realm. For the moment the role of Verica and Togidubnus was most valuable on the diplomatic front, reconciling some wavering groups amongst their own Atrebates to the over-whelming benefits of the new order.

The frontier in the west lay upon the southern section of the Fosse Way, the frontier and line of communication (*limes*), which, within a few years, ran almost in a straight line all the way from Exeter to Lincoln. On the Fosse itself, there were important cavalry forts, notably at Bath and Cirencester, which have both yielded tombstones of auxiliary cavalrymen on horseback. From Bath comes the stele of the Spaniard Lucius Vitellius Tancinus (*RIB* 159) whose three names show he was a Roman citizen, as does that of the Frisian Sextus Valerius Genialis, from the Frisiavones of Gallia Belgica (*RIB* 109) at Cirencester. Cirencester has also produced the tombstone of Dannicus from Germania Superior (*RIB* 108). All three monuments which may date to a few years after the initial establishment of these forts show these men, Roman provincials, riding down 'barbarians', taking part in the mythic contest between light and darkness as had the heroes of the past. To the north of the River Thames a system of tracks ran between Cirencester and Verulamium. This likewise was a frontier road (*limes*), which continued in use and is now known as Akeman Street. Recently an important fortress just south of the road and partly underlying the Roman town of Alchester, Oxfordshire has been excavated by Eberhard Sauer. Dendrochronological (tree-ring) dates from the timbers of one of the gates of what now appears to be the annexe estimate its construction to the

11 Aureus of the Emperor Claudius (reverse) celebrating the 'conquest' of Britain. Photo: the Late Ralph Merrifield

autumn of 44, although it would seem likely that there were camps in the region several months before that. An interesting find, again related to cavalry, is a glass intaglio from a signet ring showing the head of a horse within a border provided by the curved military trumpet or *cornu*. This was, in all likelihood, the seal of a cavalry *cornicen*. It used to be thought there was also a fort at Verulamium, but the finds of military equipment there largely come from native contexts and suggest that the owners might have been natives serving in the Roman army, very much the likes of Tancinus, Genialis and Dannicus though these all came from other provinces.

Dio's highly abbreviated account (lx, 19-22), river crossing and all, shows the same skilful use of *topoi*, traditional features of descriptions of campaigns, which we find being employed in accounts of the Boudican revolt and Agricola's so-called victory of Mons Graupius. A few facts can be gathered from it; in the event Togodumnus was killed and Caratacus was driven to seek sanctuary amongst the Silures. Everything was prepared for Claudius to come to Britain and claim the credit for what was in fact more a coup than a conquest. It seems that by August, coins were already being struck in Alexandria proclaiming Claudius as Conqueror of Britain. Thus, his two-week visit to Britain cannot have occurred much later than June.

12 Surviving portion of the Inscription from Claudius' Triumphal Arch at Rome

By the time that Plautius diplomatically called for 'help' from the Emperor, he and his vast entourage, ladies of the court, senators, civil servants, physicians including the famous empiricist Scribonius Largus, and entertainers must already have been well on their way. With them there were, of course, tons of supplies considered essential for the trip including many boatloads of wine, olive oil, fish sauce, figs, dates and every delicacy that the commander in chief might need for his short holiday. Most vital of all were the elephants with their trainers, to ensure that the 'durbar' achieved its intended climax. Claudius had many admirable qualities, as a scholar and administrator; even as a strategist he certainly had flair. But as an active soldier he was an embarrassment. Alexander's triumphal ride through Persepolis was doubtless played out in farce at Camulodunum as Claudius' elephant stumbled over the battlements of the old oppidum and the emperor clung on for dear life to avoid rolling in the dirt. Fortunately the 'report' of the victory, cut on the Triumphal Arch in Rome, is elegant and dignified, if a little bombastic. It was dedicated by the Senate and People in AD 51, 'because [Claudius] received the submission of [at least eleven] British kings without any loss of honour and because he was the first to bring the tribes across Ocean under Roman sway'. Behind the rhetoric, the major achievement was entirely political and diplomatic. In Britain there seems to have been an altar to Rome and

Augustus dedicated at Camulodunum, in order to secure the allegiance of the chieftains and tribal leaders of Britain to the Emperor and the Empire through the Imperial Cult. The Temple of Divus Claudius which eventually accompanied it, was only built after Claudius' death. There were coins of course, gold aurei and silver denarii struck at Rome with '*De Britannis*' as their legend, and a representation of a triumphal arch. Other coins were minted elsewhere, including a didrachm struck at Caesarea showing the emperor in a quadriga. Less seemly was the relief from the Sebasteion of Aphrodisias in Asia Minor, showing a remarkably virile Claudius dragging a figure of Britannia by the hair. But this is how the town magistrates of a distant Greek city wanted to 'heroise' the event. It is certainly not good evidence that the Roman government was intent on raping and plundering the Britons. If Claudius had known of this piece of hyperbole he would probably have been horrified.

The proclamation of victory over Britain was, after all, merely propaganda, intended for consumption by Roman citizens and by provincials, often far away. The main aim of those directly concerned with the governance of the island itself, or at least that part of it which they then controlled, was to administer the place wisely in the Roman manner, where possible leaving power in local hands. This strategy was, indeed, very largely accomplished in central southern Britain, but success was more mixed elsewhere and it is to the government of East Anglia and the north beyond the Roman frontier as they were originally conceived that we must now briefly turn.

The territory of the fortress of the XXth Legion at Camulodunum and of the Colonia which succeeded it was quite small in area, and evidently did not comprise anything like all of the territory of the Trinovantes. It is clear, indeed, from excavations around Colchester that there was considerable native continuity especially at Gosbecks and Sheepen where the leaders of a pro-Roman faction of the tribe may have been allowed to hold sway. Beyond in Norfolk and Suffolk were the Iceni, evidently an extensive federation. Although there was a revolt *c.*AD 47 against a move to disarm the tribesmen in the governorship of Ostorius Scapula, including, evidently, some fighting in which the governor's son won the *Corona Civica* (Tacitus, *Annals* XII, 31), the Iceni continued as (or were made into) a client kingdom under King Prasutagus (Tacitus, *Annals* XIV, 31) who held the peace for over a decade. Another great friend of Rome was Cartimandua, the redoubtable queen who ruled the extensive territories of the Brigantes, occupying much of northern Britain. It was she and not the Roman army who finally captured Caratacus (*Annals* XII, 36) in AD 51 and handed him over to her Roman friends.

In central southern Britain, in East Anglia, and even in Brigantia, there was evidence of enthusiastic acceptance of the Roman way of life by the upper classes. This is, perhaps, most apparent in the Atrebatic realms and allied territories in buildings such as the so-called protopalace (i.e. first palace) at Fishbourne, perhaps an early residence for the ruling house of the tribe, and in early building activity in Silchester (the Neronian period baths) and Chichester (as attested by an inscription dedicated to Nero (*RIB* 92)). At Verulamium, the capital of the Western Catuvellauni, a king was cremated in great magnificence. On a virgin site, on a hill above the city, he was laid on an ivory bed and was immolated upon a pyre whose

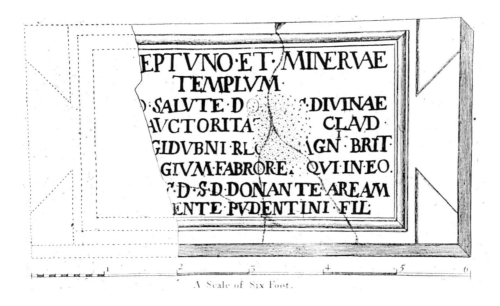

EPTVNO·ET·MINERVAE
TEMPLVM·
·SALVTE·D · ·DIVINAE
AVCTORITA·· CLAVD·
GIDVBNI·RL· ·GN·BRIT·
GIVM·FABRORE· QVI·IN·EO·
·D·S·D·DONANTE·AREAM
ENTE·PVDENTINI·FIL·

A Scale of Six Foot.

13 *Dedication of the Temple of Neptune and Minerva, Chichester*

intense heat even melted a great service of silver plate. In East Anglia, there were also significant Roman imports, again including plate, like the silver cups from Hockwold; the Roman influenced Crownthorpe cups (bronze with birds on their handles but of Roman form) and other items of metalwork show, by contrast, an attempt to assimilate Roman tastes. Even in Yorkshire the Stanwick oppidum, perhaps to be associated with Cartimandua, has yielded early samian and a small piece of a hardstone (probably chalcedony) cup.

Ultimately, it would have been hoped that the well-tried Roman system of local self-government based on cities would replace these kingdoms, but only in the south did such a process happen almost to plan and then only after a nasty shock. The death of Prasutagus in 59 was followed by a clumsy attempt to absorb his kingdom by force. The story as we have it in Tacitus suggests a Roman policy both brutal and crass. We are told that Prasutagus' widow, Boudica was flogged and her daughters raped (Tacitus, *Annals* XIV, 31). 'His kingdom was ravaged by centurions and his household by Roman slaves.' This sounds very much like an atrocity story put out later by Boudica to justify her revolt. There are modern parallels of terrorists listing similar wrongs, but the objective observer does not always believe them! In any case, would the Romans have been so crassly stupid? Interestingly, the only major tribal group who joined her was the Trinovantes, angered by the building of the *colonia* at Camulodunum and above all by the temple which the Senate had decreed to the deified Claudius in AD 54, and which they saw as the *arx aeternae dominationis*, 'the citadel of eternal domination' (Tacitus, *Annals* XIV, 31).

At first Boudica met with considerable success, by sacking and burning Colchester together with its hated temple and defeating the IXth Legion under its

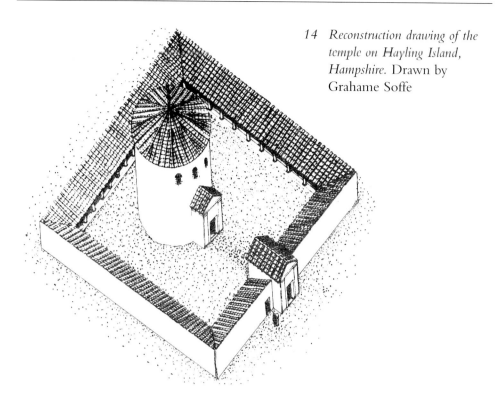

14 Reconstruction drawing of the temple on Hayling Island, Hampshire. Drawn by Grahame Soffe

impetuous commander, Petillius Cerialis. The II Augusta over in Exeter would in any case have taken some time to move against her, but the camp commandant, Poenius Postumius, did not feel able to leave the Fortress entrusted to his care. No doubt he felt that the Durotriges and the Dumnonii beyond them might revolt. The governor, Suetonius Paulinus, had been far away, campaigning in Anglesey. When he heard the shocking news he rushed south with the XIVth Gemina and the XXth Legion, but clearly not all the troops could be expected to arrive at the same time and in good order. He was not in time to save the growing community of Londinium or the Catuvellaunian capital of Verulamium from sack.

What probably happened next is a crucial element in our story. The position of Roman power in Britain was now desperate. The burning of London had cut off a reliable escape route through Kent. Two legions were in little position to help; two were exhausted (and one need only recall what happened a millennium later to King Harold's army after the Battle of Stamford Bridge, when he dashed south to meet Norman William at Senlac, near Hastings only to be defeated and slain). All Boudica needed to do was to sweep westwards and destroy the second 'collaborationist' oppidum of Calleva and then the major armies of Britain would be bottled up in the middle of Britain without hope of succour. There was another *Clades Variana* in the making. But Calleva was not sacked; instead, Boudica was defeated in battle. Although the descriptions we possess consist of characteristic *topoi*, I am often tempted to place the event in the south Chilterns, possibly at the Goring gap, where the Chilterns are only divided by the narrowed valley of the Thames from the

Berkshire Downs, which is the most dramatic scenery through which the traveller passes on the train between Oxford and Reading.

The only 'fresh' Roman troops available to oppose the revolt were vexillations guarding the supply depots at the Magnus Portus, perhaps drawn from all four legions. A tiny fragment of inscription from the dynastic temple site on Hayling Island records a soldier of Legio IX. These troops were doubtless accompanied by auxiliaries and most reassuringly by Tiberius Claudius Togidubnus, now surely king, having succeeded Verica, and described by Tacitus (*Agricola* 14) as 'totally loyal down to our own time'. He may also have had a small army of his own. It may well have been now that he showed his merit not only in keeping southern Britain friendly but by playing a crucial role in destroying Boudica. One can very probably see him, together with the new procurator Gaius Julius Alpinus Classicianus (probably, like his wife, a member of the Treveran ruling class), as a strong influence in limiting the extent of the governor's reprisals.

The Brigantian client kingdom like that of the Iceni broke up, not this time as the result of revolt but of strife between the ruling families of the confederacy. The story preserved by Tacitus has all the makings of a soap opera. Cartimandua divorced her husband Venutius and took instead his good-looking armour bearer Vellocatus (Tacitus, *Histories* III, 45). This resulted in Cartimandua being driven from her throne and forced to seek shelter with the Romans in about AD 70. 'Venutius was left with the kingdom; we the war.' In fact the account is tinged with Roman moralistic and male chauvinist ideas. Cartimandua (like Boudica in very different circumstances) is castigated as a woman in power. She had been a remarkably successful queen for 25 years or so, but the infrastructure of power was not stable enough for any sort of continuity. Life was very different in the south; in the very year in which she fell, Togidubnus came into his own.

AD 70. The Rewards of Victory.

The king had spent a nervous year. Roman armies battled across the Empire; those of Britain were not so active but tended to favour Vitellius. Togidubnus was circumspect. He was known to be a protegé, perhaps a friend of Vespasian and of his sons.

How long he could expect to keep his throne despite his brilliance in the fight against Boudica is unknown.

Then, one day, as he was talking to one of his clients, a chieftain belonging to the cadet branch of the family called Tiberius Claudius Catuarus, a fast galley put into the harbour. A senior centurion, long absent, of Legio II, dressed in fine golden armour for the occasion leapt ashore and fairly ran towards the villa. As he got nearer he saw he was carrying gilded scrolls tied by purple ribbons. His face was cheerful. 'Greetings Marcus!', called the king, reassured by the man's bearing. 'Good news sir!', he replied. 'Vitellius is dead! Our Lord Flavius Vespasianus is Emperor. I bring letters both official and unofficial. "Certain territories are being given to you" . . . that is what it says. You are as good a Roman as any of us . . . and the territories are "extensive", bounded by the Fosse to the west, Akeman Street to the north and Verulamium to the east. It leaves us with London, Colchester and trouble in the uplands. Oh, and there is a title to go with it, "*Rex Magnus Britanniae*" – "Great King in Britain" – and the Emperor suggests that this pokey little place isn't really fit for his friend, the king and gives his authorisation and some practical help to build a palace . . . he might want to stay one day.'

'What about the governor?'. The king was a little alarmed that these favours might furnish grounds for resentment. 'Vespasian has thought about that too. Watch him, whoever he is.'

This imaginary meeting explains what appears to be a remarkable lost episode in the history of Roman Britain. Togidubnus' name occurs, as we have seen, on just one inscription from Chichester. *RIB* 91 is the dedication of a temple to Neptune and Minerva in honour of the Divine House (the Imperial Family) by the authority of the king, styled 'Rex Magnus Britanniae'. The deities are interesting, representing as they do the sea and the land. As Poseidon and Athene they guarded Athens, as Togidubnus would have known. His temple-building activity did not end here; across the water at the dynastic sanctuary of Hayling Island a new stone temple was erected to replace the wooden one; it has been suggested that it might have been a temple mausoleum for Verica. The third temple was the greatest of all, the temple of Sulis Minerva at Bath. There are several reasons to attribute this temple to Togidubnus' patronage, starting with the fact that it would appear to have been within his kingdom. The geographer Ptolemy attributes Aquae Sulis to the Belgae (whose capital was Winchester), generally recognised as being within Togidubnus' enlarged realm. Then the patron of such a temple must have been a very rich man. The architecture is idiosyncratic and celticising as is the sculpture. Then the major feature of the pediment is a mask of Neptune conflated with Minerva's Medusa mask. Minerva herself is represented by an owl. The pediment with its double oak wreath, each of them a '*corona civica*', Victories standing on globes and tritons blowing conches, is full of Roman triumphal imagery. The star in the apex and another from the architrave must represent *Divus Claudius* unless they are later and date from after Vespasian's own death in AD 79, in which case they could refer to *Divus Vespasianus*, also, as we have seen, one of the heroes of the invasion or liberation of 43. In favour of this would be Domitian's especial devotion to Minerva. It would hardly be surprising to find Togidubnus erecting victory monuments for, very properly, he would have regarded himself and his people as allies of Rome, indeed as far as he and his leading compatriots were concerned, with their grants of citizenship, as fully-fledged Romans.

The other great monument associated with Togidubnus was the Fishbourne palace. Although it has been suggested by some that it was intended for the governor's palace, when could he ever have used it? Almost certainly it was intended that the governor would reside in the north and, under Agricola there seem to have been moves to build a residence for him at Chester. Recently a fine gold signet ring inscribed in large block capitals for Tiberius Claudius Catuarus has been found here,

15a Cella *of temple on Hayling Island under excavation.* Photo: Grahame Soffe

15b Cella *of Temple of Vesunna at Périgueux in Gaul*

16   Details from pediment of the Temple of Sulis Minerva, Bath. a Head of Neptune
conflated with Minerva's emblem, the Medusa. Note the corona civica and Minerva's
owl; b Victory on globe. Photos: Institute of Archaeology, Oxford

suggesting a powerful local Briton, a citizen of at least Equestrian rank, and probably a kinsman of the Great King. The first palace, Neronian in date, was fairly small, though furnished in a stylish manner and with what may have been an imposing temple near its entrance. This structure (building 3) survived its extensive Flavian rebuild as a villa with the ground area if not the mass of the Flavian palace in Rome. Here was surely a major 'centre of lordship'. The villa had many ranges of rooms around a vast garden court replete with fountains, Its interiors were of exceptional magnificence with room after room of mosaic pavements, mainly geometrical in character, and wall veneers of marble and coloured stone, together with wall paintings and stucco. There was, undoubtedly, marble statuary (a head plausibly of Togidubnus as a child remains), elaborate furniture with gilt and niello inlay; and, to judge by the finding of the handle of a water jug or *askos* with an escutcheon in the form of a young satyr, finely cast in bronze and embellished with silvering, the vessels used at table were rare and expensive. The luxurious setting and finds like the gold signet ring of Tiberius Claudius Catuarus and some very fine intaglios from rings which are discussed below, all suggest a *domus* owned by a very special person indeed. This was a luxury palace of a type more at home on the bay of Naples, though there are a number of smaller examples, villas built at the same time along the coast of Sussex and Hampshire, at Pulborough, Angmering and Southwick for example. In these *domus* resided Togidubnus' loyal followers, the Atrebatic nobles of the vicinity, one of whom might have been Catuarus.

It is possible that there was yet another luxurious, royal building a mile or two along the coast to the west, at Bosham. Evidence for this lies in some of the building materials incorporated in the late Saxon church which include blocks of Ditrupa limestone from near Paris, a stone also used at Fishbourne. There are also pieces of wall plaster from beside the church. Even more telling is a colossal head of Trajan. It is not known whether Togidubnus died before Trajan's reign began in AD 98, but it is likely that the statue from which it came was installed by him or by his heirs. A bronze thumb hints at another Imperial statue. Most interesting of all is the discovery, a century and a half ago, of a marble head of Germanicus, older brother to Claudius, and held in high regard by the emperor.

Together with these we should consider the striking circular temple on Hayling Island which certainly goes back to the first century BC. This was rebuilt in the Flavian period in well-coursed stone of the same build as the Fishbourne palace. The entrance loggia was provided with black and white mosaics like those of Fishbourne (though only a few loose tesserae remain). The tower-like structure in the centre must have been visible from afar, as the temple of Vesunna at Périgueux is today. Almost certainly this was a dynastic building and perhaps a Royal mausoleum, analogous to the Catuvellaunian temple-tomb built at Folly Lane, Verulamium, on the site of the royal cremation there. Of course Roman temples (like that at Bath or the temple of Neptune and Minerva in Chichester) would not have allowed the presence of dead bodies within their precincts, which would have brought pollution. Despite its Romanising architecture, the Hayling monument was something rather different, and represented a native aspect of the king's rule.

17a Star on architrave of Temple of Sulis Minerva.
Photo: Institute of Archaeology, Oxford

17b Similar star on denarius of Julius Caesar. Photo: Ashmolean Museum

18a   Fishbourne palace. Reception room in west wing under excavation

18b   Hydraulic pipes in garden

19 Life-size marble head of Germanicus, brother of Claudius, found in 1851 at Bosham, Hampshire

Those tempted to regard client kingship as being the same as puppet kingship, or to see the Roman involvement in Britain as fundamentally exploitative should consider Togidubnus and his realm. This was not, in any sense, a 'Bantustan' or, as Tacitus unjustly hints (*Agricola* 14), 'a means of making even kings Roman agents in enslaving their people'; it was the very heartland of Britain agriculturally and with the potential of remaining the cultural core of the Province. The question to be asked here is not, 'how was the province conquered?', but 'how did it become Roman?'. The correct modern name for Togidubnus' realm is a 'protectorate', only in this particular case, as we have seen, that word has a rather unexpected resonance, as it had been the king and his tribesmen who played a key role in protecting the land for the Roman Empire.

How to become a Roman

The most famous chapter in Tacitus' *Agricola* (ch. 21) is concerned not with warfare but with civilian developments. Admittedly Agricola is given the full credit for assistance in public works, education and fashion, but we have seen evidence that leading Roman Britons had voluntarily become Romans before Agricola. Certainly the porticos, baths and banquets – was Tacitus sneering at Fishbourne? – were what characterised the lives of well to do Romans in Italy as well as Britain. For the

20 *Twice life-size head of the Emperor Trajan from Bosham.* Photo: Grahame Soffe

historian the choice is between the freedom of the Britons before the Conquest and the servitude of the provincial. However, as noted above, the freedom to live the good life was severely compromised for many in endemic warfare and fear of enslavement which in central southern Britain was ended by the Claudian expedition. Civilisation (*humanitas*) was an expression of culture, of refinement. It is well exemplified by a friend of the poet Martial, a British lady living in Rome, called Claudia Rufina (*Epigr.* 11.53), surely related to one of the British dynasts.

Literacy was of primary importance. It allowed individuals to express their personalities in religious dedications like a certain Lucullus, the son of a man called Ammin(i)us, the name the same as Cunobelin's pro-Roman son, who set up an altar to the Genius Loci at Chichester. Spirit of place is apparent in the choice of Brucetus' son named Sulinus after Sulis Minerva who made offerings to deities called the Suleviae at Cirencester and Bath. Tombstones provide a record of lives which had become increasingly Roman. Catia, who was the wife or daughter of Censorinus at Chichester and lived to be 23 (*RIB* 95), possibly has a local, Atrebatic name, for a kinsman of Togidubnus who perhaps lived at Fishbourne had a signet ring inscribed with his Roman name Tiberius Claudius Catuarus, the cognomen having the Celtic root Catu-. Is it possible that the armourer of Legio XX, Julius Vitalis, *natione Belga*, serving for nine years before dying at Bath at the age of 29 (*RIB* 156), came from only a short distance to the west, for the Belgae were a local tribe, whose capital was established at *Venta* (Winchester)? Within his unit, the armourer's guild financed his funeral.

According to Thomas Hobbes in his *Leviathan*, the life of man in a state of nature, that is freed from organised society, was inevitably 'solitary, poor, nasty, brutish and short'. Society in the Roman Empire was organised, not only through family but through relations with protectors (patrons) and dependants (clients), designed to be beneficial. Togidubnus was a client of Claudius but, on the one inscription which names him, he seems himself to be a patron of a guild of smiths (*RIB* 91). Such guilds

21 *Julius Agricola a Roman Governor in Britain under the Emperor Domitian introducing the Roman Arts and Sciences into England, the inhabitants of which are astonished and soon become fond of the Arts and manners of their cruel invaders'.* From Edward Barnard's *History of England (c.1791)*

were quite widespread: the treasurer of another guild set up a dedication to the *Matres Domesticae* again at Chichester, while Silchester supported a guild of 'foreigners' (*peregrini*) (*RIB* 69-71). The most significant corporations were the groupings of leading men who ran the town halls, for example the *ordo* of Verulamium which perhaps came into being during Agricola's governorship as the forum inscription from that city proclaims.

Making a record of oneself, at its simplest level, was a matter of writing on papyrus or, in Britain, more usually on thin sheets of wood. Even though little survives from civilian Britain apart from a few scraps from business letters and legal contracts, we have numerous traces of literacy, in styli, seal-boxes which protected the imprint of seals and above all signets themselves. With regard to the latter inscribed names are altogether exceptional, but devices expressed not just individual personality but cultural aspirations. It is never possible to be certain about ownership. Scenes of battling Greek heroes appear to have had especial appeal within the Roman army, but some may have been owned by civilians. Finds of engraved gems from Fishbourne are especially interesting giving as they do some idea of taste in the circle of Togidubnus. The device of a racehorse with a palm of victory on a nicolo-onyx is suggestive of a passion for chariot racing, not surprising here; this example is, incidentally, one of the best cut examples of the type ever found, as befits its exceptional

22a   Cornelian intaglio from Bath depicting a discobolus, height 12.5mm

22b   Green chalcedony intaglio from Bath showing Methe, the personification of Drunkenness. Height 10mm. Photos: Institute of Archaeology, Oxford

CATIA
CENSoRIN
AN XXIII

23 Tombstone of Catia from Chichester, Sussex

findspot and ownership. Another superb intaglio, far superior to the average in its workmanship, is an amethyst showing the god Mercury leaning against a column. The elder Pliny tells us that some of his contemporaries thought amethysts were useful if approaching a king as a suppliant, but it is possibly more likely that the supposed prophylactic qualities of the stone against drunkenness were more significant here. No doubt the little gold ring containing a minute chrome chalcedony depicting a bird was a child's ring. The material of the ring (like Catuarus' ring, likewise of gold) demonstrates the high rank of those who lived in this great *domus*. In nearby Chichester a sard intaglio portrays a sphinx, a type which was once used by the Emperor Augustus himself as his signet, until his enemies pointed out the creature's devious character. Another mythological type is a chrome chalcedony intaglio depicting the unfortunate satyr, Marsyas, who was defeated by Apollo in a musical contest. His double pipes rest, now useless, against a rock. We know he is about to be flayed for his presumption. Such myth scenes are a reminder of the way Classical myth was fully understood and accepted in the higher circles of society, a theme which will be taken up at length later in the book.

From Bath a cache of 34 intaglios found in uncertain circumstances in digging out the main drain, so it is not certain whether they were a votive offering in the spring or losses by bathers, give a good idea of aspirations at this period. There are not only a circus scene and two gems showing chariots but Greek athletics is represented by a discobolos. Such non-Roman practices were rather frowned on by conservatives who feared they would encourage homosexuality amongst the young, but it is clear that such activities were very much part of the culture of the palaestra; they persisted even in military circles, as a bronze plaque showing two athletes and a discus on a stand was found at Caerleon. An old gem dating from the first century BC and of Greek workmanship was found at the villa at North Cerney near Corinium. It depicts a nude youth standing by a herm.

Many of the Bath intaglios depict cupids, sometimes clearly regarded as representing the wine-god Bacchus, also represented by gems showing a satyr and a panther. There is

24 Jupiter monument from Chichester: a inscription; b side showing two water nymphs.
   Photos: Grahame Soffe

also a figure of Methe, the goddess of intoxication; this was notoriously the subject of Queen Cleopatra VII's signet, suitable for a hedonistic queen who evidently used an amethyst to counteract the effects of Methe's power! The Bath gem is, alas, not an amethyst but a green chrome-chalcedony. There are also some delightful animal studies: a mastiff, horses, an ass, and a group of three cows. What is clear from such personal objects is that humour and a certain frivolity were very much in evidence in Britain as they were in Pompeii.

The remains of Togidubnus' capital, *Noviomagus*, the 'new market' (now Chichester), which had replaced the old dispersed oppidum are not very well known, despite a bold series of excavations by the late Alec Down. This is largely because a very fine Georgian city now overlies it. One or two town houses with mosaics have been found (one of them under the East End of the Cathedral) but they are subsequent to his time. However, it would seem that some civic buildings went up in his reign including public baths (in Tower Street) and possibly even the forum though Alec Down places its construction after his death. For prestige purposes an amphitheatre was built outside the town. Amongst religious structures, in addition to the temple of Neptune and Minerva, there was the base of a monument to Jupiter 'Greatest and Best' in honour of the *Domus Divina* (the Imperial Family (*RIB* 89)). On one side are shown two water nymphs; on others Minerva and perhaps Apollo, but originally further deities would assuredly have been shown on other levels of the structure. In the same general area in the centre of the city was the altar to the Genius (the *Genius Loci* no doubt) dedicated, as noted above, by Lucullus (*RIB* 90). Very probably there was an associated statue of the god, whose head-dress represented a city wall showing that the Genius personified the city itself. Also possibly dating to this time is the dedication by an arkarius or gild-treasurer to the *Matres Domesticae* ('Mothers of the Homeland'), a cult probably brought in from Germany and a reminder of the cosmopolitan nature of the King's realm. Bath too attracted visitors from other Western provinces as well as soldiers. A 'Great King' took such diversity in his stride.

A meditation by the King. AD 95.

I am an old man now, almost as old as Verica lived to be. I became his sole heir. As I walk through my grand, formal gardens, lit by the western, evening sun, enjoying the perfume of my roses, watching the gardeners take cuttings in their special planters, imported from Italy, and sometimes helping them, I reflect on my wonderful good fortune, even at times when I thought I was in mortal danger. I listen to the birdsong, both the free birds, and those I keep in the aviary, and take enormous pleasure in the splashing waters from the many fountains around the place. The engineering that brings these ever-living waters to me is superb. That rather nice, scholarly governor, Julius Frontinus, once explained it all but I have to confess it was too technical for me to understand.

I watch my grandchildren at play in the orchard, joking with each other in Latin. My son is very proud to have been made a quinquennalis yesterday; he was elected to one of the two magistracies which the constitution provides for, selected once every four years to help revise the electoral list of Noviomagus. When he was small he wanted to be a 'king' like me and wear a diadem like that Herod Agrippa I told him about. I spoke more seriously to him when he brought it up a few years later and said that my Roman friends would not like it, and in any case we were Romans now. People can so easily get the wrong idea of monarchy, like that dreadful harpy Boudica. Even Herod Agrippa came unstuck. I was never tempted to take the way of rebellion against Caesar any more than I could have been tempted to blaspheme Jupiter. Anyway I became king for my people, who will henceforth rule themselves, and, I trust, very well. Sometimes, presiding over a feast for my own clients, I am still expected to act the Celtic king, dressing to excess with torques and armbands of gold, making a show of drinking much more than everyone else, being lavish with gifts and generally 'playing the barbarian'. I do that less and less now, and never when I have visitors from Italy. It is distasteful to me: first and foremost, as I told my son, I am a Roman, a beneficiary of Roman culture and a representative of it in Britain. It was different when my uncle was king. What alternative did we have to living in huts and acting as barbarians?

The gods have certainly always been very kind to me. As a boy I saw my land taken and ravaged by invaders from Camulodunum. I went to the Capitol with my offerings and asked Jupiter, Best and Greatest for his aid. My patron Claudius – the Divine Claudius I should say – got it back for us. I think of Aeneas driven out of Troy, an exile, buffeted by the sea and at last coming home. Vergil understood the bitterness of becoming an outcast. That is why the *Aeneid* is my favourite poem: its story is my story too. Noviomagus is my Alba Longa. I wonder where our British Rome will be?

You know, after that feisty lady, Queen Cartimandua, had captured Caratacus she handed him over to Claudius, who actually pardoned him and gave him a house in Italy. Before he did so, he wrote to me and asked me to decide Caratacus' fate. I thought for a moment or two; then three lines from the sixth book of the *Aeneid* came into my mind:

'tu regere imperio populos, Romane, memento
(haec tibi erunt artes) pacique imponere morem,
parcere subiectis et debellare superbos.'

'O Roman, remember to rule the nations with might. This will be your genius – to impose the way of peace, to spare the humbled and to crush the proud.'

I knew at once, instinctively, that my friend Claudius was right to be magnanimous. Not to have agreed with him would have been to show myself a barbarian. Magnanimity is always the true way. Suetonius Paulinus sought the way of revenge on Boudica, and Classicianus had my full support in writing in the strongest possible terms to Nero on the matter, and Suetonius was justly (though diplomatically) removed. Plato commends clemency to his philosopher king. Claudius, in his way, was such a ruler and he deserved his divinity. I will never forget his support and friendliness to me as a boy. Go to Bath and see, I have placed his star in the apex of the pediment of the temple of Sulis, and I hope he can see it.

In the last thirty years I have had far more power, far more influence in the world, than any past ruler of the Atrebates – even Commius – and I hope I have used it wisely for the honour of Britain and of Rome. I have tried to repay the gods too. Jupiter, Neptune and Minerva here; Sulis Minerva at Bath. There the sanctuary and baths will be my enduring memorial and legacy, healing the sick and providing relaxation, *otium*, for the living; and I like to think that long centuries from now, men, women and children will still be bathing there in those warm, sulphurous waters and praising the beneficence of the divine powers.

The world into which I was born was a dark, tribal world. Chieftains bragged about the sharpness of their swords, the showiness of their shields and scabbards, they drank . . . and how they drank, and they quarrelled. They lived in smelly round huts with pigs and cattle. Men were sacrificed like sheep and life was cheap. Now my grand-children learn beautiful poems, read history, study philosophy, rhetoric, mathematics. Claudia Rufina has been a great hit in Rome, more for her wit, it seems, than her red hair. Even the dimensions of the palace and of the temples of my realm are metaphors for an ideal symmetry and order in the cosmos. As a Briton and a Roman I know I have liberated my people from ignorance, warfare and the persecution of one tribe by another. Without the emperors of Rome, especially my dear friends Divus Claudius, Divus Vespasianus, Divus Titus and the still-reigning emperor, his brother Domitian, it could not, I think, have been done.

When I die I ask no more than that my body lies in our sacred island at Hayling alongside the body of my uncle Verica, where the high white tower of the temple-mausoleum which I have rebuilt acts as a lighthouse to the kingdom and will continue to protect the old civitas and keep it tranquil. Time and again I return to the old wisdom of the Greeks. In *Oedipus at Colonus*, Sophocles writes of his own land, protected for ever more by the bones of King Oedipus in his secret resting place. I find that idea a comforting one...May all those who come after me, and live in this beautiful land of ours, remember old Togidubnus with kindness . . .

But that is a morbid, introspective way to think of oneself! Old Claudius (what a way to think of a god!, but I am remembering him when he was just a bookish scholar in the library teaching a small foreign boy Greek) . . . Old Claudius got me to read a bit of Greek philosophy and I was hooked by Plato. Claudius himself with his slightly unprepossessing features was my Socrates. When he became Emperor the sculptors disguised this and you won't see his facial tick on the statues; but who cares? It is the inner man who is important. I have read the *Phaedo*, and believe with Plato and his Socrates, that the soul lives on. I hope and pray that mine can approach the gods without too much reproach. I hope, in any case, to be a bit more than a Genius Loci. If I do have to be such a Genius, I would like to be somewhere where happy people congregate, presiding over a racetrack, perhaps. I have always loved horses. There is the Celt in me, venerating our sacred animal! Maybe someone will get round to building a proper hippodrome at Noviomagus; I never got round to it, myself. Perhaps that is my greatest reproach!

3 Britain and the Roman army

Are all thy conquests, glories, triumphs, spoils,
Shrunk to this little measure?

The words of Mark Antony viewing the lifeless corpse of Caesar deserve to be
echoed by those who survey the military history of Roman Britain.

It is not just the modern historian of Roman Britain or his – almost always his –
predecessors who should be sceptical and usually isn't, but one wonders what a
schoolboy might have made of it in Antiquity, a schoolboy with his wits about him
in say AD 250.

Corinium, a small school off the forum. April. AD 250.

A sharp gust blew through the portico on that spring day, not many weeks after the
official start of the campaigning season. Primus gathered his Gallic coat around him. At
least the cold kept him awake, and the lesson was becoming rather interesting. He was
studying the stories of ancient battles in Livy, with a view to being able to compose his
own accounts of conflicts between gods and giants, Greeks and Trojans, Romans and
Carthaginians. The trick was to find what his master, old Strato, a Greek freedman called
'topoi. Strato said that the old Greek writers did the same thing. 'Think of geography!'
The master pointed. 'Over there are the Cotswold hills, rising and falling . . . Make them
bigger if you like. Then put in a river, a marsh, or a forest. Vary the description. Find a
likely name for the leader of a barbarian tribe. Then put Achilles into the picture. Both
give speeches before the battle. Put the longer odds on Achilles. But make him win!'

Primus was impressed. 'Is it true?'

'Of course it is!', said Strato, 'You are the historian; it is your task to make it true,
for those who read it. The Greek writer Lucian wrote an amusing "True history"
about a trip to the moon to show people what historians get up to, and I expect quite
a lot of his readers believed him . . .'

'Could we make a "true history" here?'. Primus wondered if anything special had
ever happened in Britain, this land at the far end of the world, as it had happened far
away on the shores of the warm Mediterranean. Rome was miles away and though
Strato said he had been born in Greece and seen Delphi, Primus did not know
whether that was an invention too.

'Yes, indeed, my boy', replied Strato, 'and as you have been very good, we will look
together at some extracts from a modern historian – he lived only a 100 years or so

ago in the days of Trajan and Hadrian. His name was Tacitus. He wrote about everything that happened to the glory of the Roman period from the death of Augustus to the death of Domitian. He had quite a bit to say about Britain on the way , the "conquest", the rebellion of Boudica, the expansion to the north . . . and we find that a large part of this "conquest" was the work of a great governor called Agricola who just happened to be his father-in-law. Afterwards the emperor Domitian gave up some of the territory in which Agricola built his fortress and forts and Tacitus comments that "Britain was thoroughly conquered and immediately let go!" Tacitus was angry because this Agricola was a relative. He wrote a short book in praise of Agricola too. If you read that you will see a real master of "*topoi*", weaving in just the right amount of detail to make a plausible and gripping story. This Tacitus was a real Roman aristocrat, though with a bit of Gaul in him! The trouble is the Britons on the whole don't come out of his history too well unless they are savage barbarians like Boudica. People like your great uncle who built the baths here are, for him, little better than slaves!'

'He was a stuck-up liar!' shouted Primus, loyal as always to his distinguished family.

'Perhaps', agreed Strato. 'Although he was educated in the Greek city of Massilia, he does not seem to have had a lot of time for Greeks either. Still he was a wonderful historian, a skilled craftsman with words. And he was writing for Roman senators in Rome. Remember that those aristocrats in Rome see Britain as the setting for a sort of modern Trojan War . . . their very own "Trojan War" in fact; and when their young men come over to fight what do they put on their signet rings? Achilles, of course, or Diomedes seizing the Palladium from Troy . . . as though they themselves were ancient Greeks! In fact our legends say that the Romans are Trojans, descended from refugees. A more truthful person would show Aeneas fleeing Troy with his son and aged father. But did that War really and truly take place anyway, at least in the way Homer tells it to us?'

Primus reflected. 'So, "history" is a way of passing down what you want to pass down to future generations. The phrase "to states unborn and peoples yet unknown" comes to mind.'

'You could put it like that!', concurred Strato with a laugh.

If the setting of this conversation is imaginary, the criticism I have put into the mouth of Strato remains valid. Although details of topography in the surviving account of 'the conquest' (which we have already seen was not entirely a conquest), of Boudica's defeat and Agricola's great victory at the Battle of Mons Graupius are made up of stock descriptions it is very tempting for those of us who live in the British Isles to locate the scenes of these conflicts. As this book is not concerned with the Roman Army as such but with the culture of Roman Britain not a great deal need be said of these campaigns.

In its essentials, as we have already seen, the conquest of 43 was a coup which could be presented in Rome, Caesarea, Alexandria, Aphrodisias and anywhere else on coins and triumphal monuments as Claudius' great victory; even the Boudican

1a   The Great Garden at the Roman palace of Fishbourne, Sussex

1b   Gallica roses and 1c Autumn damask roses were probably grown here

2a   Painting of seaside villa, Fishbourne.
Photo: Institute of Archaeology,
Oxford

2b   City wall mosaic, Fishbourne (detail).
Photo: Grahame Soffe

2c   Monochrome geometric mosaic, Fishbourne. Photo: Institute of Archaeology, Oxford

3a Bracelet and gold
    signet ring from
    early first-century
    hoard, Alton,
    Hants. Photo:
    British Museum

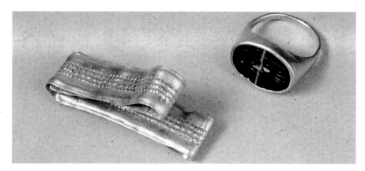

3b Nicolo intaglio from Fishbourne
    showing a racehorse, length
    10mm. Photo: Institute of
    Archaeology, Oxford

3c Gilt bronze furniture fitting
    from Fishbourne, diameter
    29mm. Photo: courtesy of
    the late Alec Down

3d Chrome chalcedony
    intaglio showing
    Marsyas, from
    Chichester, Sussex,
    length 17mm.
    Photo: Institute
    of Archaeology,
    Oxford

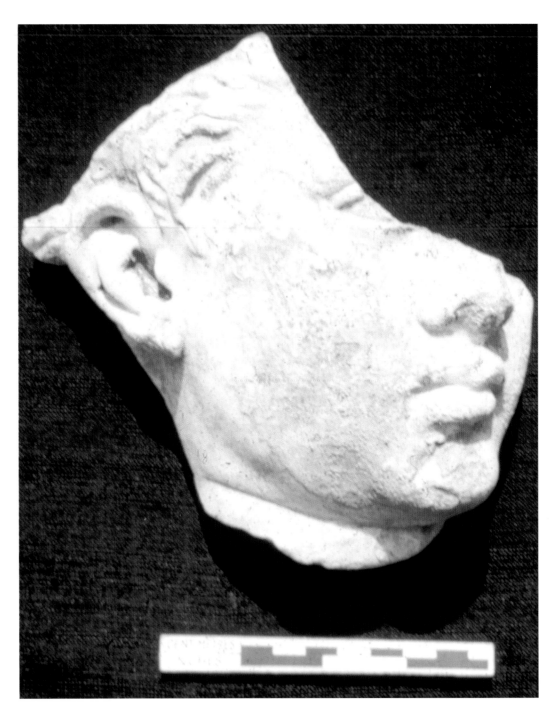

4 Marble head of boy, perhaps Togidubnus as he looked c.AD 42.
Photo: Institute of Archaeology, Oxford

5a/b *Bronze sestertius of the Emperor Vespasian. The reverse shows the Corona Civica*

5c *Exotic marble veneers from Fishbourne.* All photos: Institute of Archaeology, Oxford

6a   Actaeon torn to pieces by his own hounds, second-century mosaic from Cirencester

6b   Cyparissus and the stag from Leicester. Photos: Institute of Archaeology, Oxford

7 *Details of mosaics from Frampton, Dorset (by Samuel Lysons).*

a *Aeneas plucks the Golden Bough*

b *Attis with the nymph Sangaritis*

c *Neptune and dolphins juxtaposed with the chi-rho*

8a   Temple of Nodens, Lydney, Gloucestershire

8b   Mosaic from cella of Temple of Nodens

9   Details of mosaics at Bignor (by Samuel Lysons) a Venus

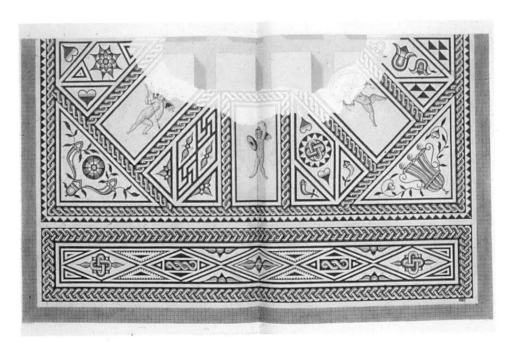

b   Cupids with shields (servants to Mars?) on contiguous floor

10 *Details of mosaics at Bignor (by Samuel Lysons).*
a *Ganymede and the eagle*

b *Dancing maenads(?) on contiguous floor*

11 Details of mosaics
at Brading, Isle of
Wight.

a The Holy Man or
'astronomer'.
Photo:
Grahame Soffe

b The cock-headed man
(Abraxas or Hermes
Trismegistos?) with
griffins.
Photo: Institute of
Archaeology,
Oxford

c Perseus and Andromeda.
Photo: Institute of
Archaeology,
Oxford

12 Bacchus mosaic from Thruxton, Hampshire (by John Lickman).
Photo: courtesy of Grahame Soffe

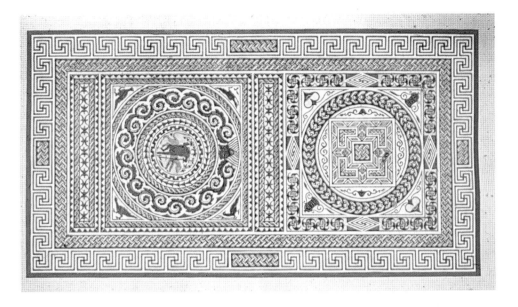

13a   Bacchus mosaic from Stonesfield, Oxfordshire (coloured engraving, George Vertue)

13b   Red jasper intaglio found near Gloucester showing Socrates, length 12mm

14a Silver gilt cockerel from Cirencester, length 32mm

14b Nicolo intaglio from Woodeaton, Oxfordshire depicting a squirrel, length 12mm

14c Onyx cameo from villa at North Wraxall, Wiltshire depicting clasped hands and inscribed in Greek, 'Good Fortune . . . Harmony!', length 13.5mm.
All photos: Institute of Archaeology, Oxford

15 The Great
   Pavement,
   Woodchester,
   Gloucestershire.
a General view
   of half the
   pavement by S.
   Lysons

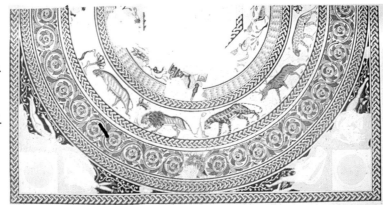

b Detail of
   griffin from
   processional
   frieze of
   quadrupeds

c Detail of dove
   from frieze of
   birds.
   b and c
   photos:
   Institute of
   Archaeology,
   Oxford

16a The temple of Uley (Nymsfield), Gloucestershire under excavation. Note the replacement or descendant of the original 'nemet' or sacred grove beyond

16b View from the Lydney temple, south across the Severn sea

25 *Tombstone of the auxiliary cavalryman Sextus Genialis, from Cirencester (detail).*
Photo: M. Cookson, Institute of Archaeology, Oxford archive

revolt resulted in a victory of sorts for Nero's legions, at least it was presented as such at Corinth where a priesthood celebrated Nero's prowess in Britain. The northern campaigns of Petillius Cerealis, Julius Frontinus and Julius Agricola arose out of necessity, the collapse of the Brigantian confederacy. While tangible gains could be made in the fine agricultural country of the vale of York, the control of wild uplands brought much less obvious benefit save in propaganda terms.

In the Flavian period lowland Britain saw a spate of town building, as an urban ruling class established itself in cities scattered across the south of England and even the Midlands. Essentially, as in Gaul, settled by Augustus three quarters of a century before these curiales were the ruling class of the province. They were the 'friends' Caesar could trust and it was for them that the Roman Empire existed. Togidubnus was merely the forerunner of their success.

While the soldiers in the north were battling to achieve a stable frontier, there were two other reasons for an immensely strong military presence up there. The first was to 'win' victories for Rome, the reports of such successes in battle being essential for the reputation of the Emperor and the regime in general. The second, unspoken, reason was that a busy army could not cause trouble by rioting or, at worst, marching on Rome.

It is natural to focus on Agricola because, thanks to Tacitus, we know rather more about him and his ethos than we do about any other governor. Agricola's character comes through from the pages of Tacitus' encomium. He was fired by the thought of glory very much by his exposure to letters, Greek as well as Roman, at the University of Massilia. As a young man, at the time of the Boudican revolt, he had been a military tribune, and some 10 years later (*c.*71-3) he was legionary legate of the Twentieth legion under the dashing but impetuous Cerealis. After a short spell as governor of Aquitaine (74-6) and the consulate in Rome, he became governor of Britain in AD 77.

In his civil administration, Agricola will have followed the policy laid down by Vespasian and executed by his predecessors as well as the tireless client king. It is hard not to imagine that certain tensions must have existed between them. Both were in a sense clients of the Emperor and drew their authority from him, but Togidubnus' remit was civil and *de facto* confined to the south. Agricola was expected to spend most of the year with the legions.

In recent years attention has been directed to the great legionary fortress at Chester. It was almost certainly begun by Frontinus for Legio II Adiutrix but on an extravagant scale, and it is possible that it was designed to be additionally the headquarters of the governor. A large central administrative building and an elliptical 'Sebasteion', a proto-Pantheon as centre for official cult, were planned. The central fountain of the latter was fed by lead pipes bearing the name of Agricola under whom the work proceeded. Tacitus records Agricola's desire to subdue Ireland which he thought he could do with a single legion. Whether this was part of Imperial policy or a thought which developed in the governnor's own mind we do not know. In any case the idea was abandoned and Agricola's enthusiasm for this field of glory channelled north.

Details of Agricola's campaigns are sparse, but archaeological evidence exists in forts built by him at this time. The climax at the end of Agricola's governorship in the reign of Domitian was the notorious Battle of Mons Graupius. The splendour of Tacitus' narrative and the setting in or on the edge of the Scottish Highlands has made it central to much Romano-British military archaeology and historical-topography, especially north of the border. But did a pitched battle between Romans and Britons ever actually take place?

In Tacitus' account we begin with the speech of the British leader Calgacus, whose name at least sounds authentic; he rallies his men with a great speech about *libertas* and the duplicity of the Romans. 'Theft, butchery, rape, the liars call it "Empire"; they create a wasteland and call it "peace".' At the dinner parties in Rome where this speech was declaimed, there would have been much applause amongst cognoscenti who had perhaps themselves written speeches at school, for Achilles preferring honour and death over long life with dishonour. Agricola responds, telling his troops that with the forthcoming battle all of Britain will be theirs. So it will prove. The Roman combatants comprise auxiliary infantry and cavalry, but not legionaries. 'Victory would be much more glorious if no Romans were killed'. The battle is described, a matter of literary artifice. Ten thousand of the enemy die to only 360 on the Roman side, including, however, Aulus Atticus, the prefect of a cohort.

26 *Bronze head of Hadrian from London, height 42cm.* After C. Roach Smith, *Illustrations of Roman London*, 1859

The truth may have been considerably more prosaic. It is most unlikely that in a mountainous setting the Britons would have congregated for a pitched battle. Instead they would have fallen back and waited for the Roman armies to exhaust themselves as supply lines became ever more extended and winter set in. There would doubtless have been a few insignificant skirmishes; Mons Graupius may have been one of these. Victory could no doubt have been proclaimed by both Agricola and 'Calgacus' in these circumstances, but Agricola had a far better propaganda machine. 'Victory' in Britain may have been celebrated in Britain itself by the big, marble-clad arch at Richborough, the 'gateway to Britain', the '*accessus Britanniae*' and certainly, as already mentioned, at Bath.

Tacitus, hostile to Domitian, in part because of his failure to reward his father-in-law adequately with another prestige posting, makes him receive the news with joy on his face masking secret disquiet. However, we do not need to follow Tacitus in ascribing a sinister motive to this. Agricola, largely undisturbed by the enemy in the heather of the Highlands, after a campaign which left him in control (apparently) of large tracts of territory, built a fortress for a legion, possibly the Twentieth, at Inchtuthil in Perthshire. The problem for the Romans was that lines of communication were impossibly extended. How would a site 200 miles north of York continue to be supplied with food, wine and other necessities? Was there any chance of attracting civilian investment in the hinterland? It was certainly a 'fortress too far'.

Domitian might well have been worried for some time. Expansion of the Empire to take in Ireland or Highland Scotland played no part in the sensible ordering of affairs. He would have had reports from the Procurator on the cost implications but possibly the most detailed and reliable would have come from Togidubnus, a long-standing, totally reliable friend of the family. Let us imagine the tenor of the intelligence he received:

[Top Secret] My Lord and Friend, Your Legate is, of course, far away, but I have a good servant, a trader in fine wines who has managed to get into the good offices of the Legate's steward. I have no reason to believe that Agricola is bent on treason but he does think he is Achilles and was heard wondering whether having totally conquered Britain, he might end up as governor of Asia and subdue the Parthian Empire. You remember Ireland: my kinsman Catuarus went there, at your suggestion, to check whether there really were vast goldmines there. There aren't . . . but lots of bogs and you would need three legions for nothing . . . Agricola needed to be diverted . . . Now the mutt has built a fortress for a legion at some spot forsaken by all the gods, miles from anywhere and my friend had enormous difficulty getting an ox-cart of Falernian to him. He says no way would he do it if he was acting 'commercially'.

I am trying to be just to Julius Agricola. He isn't a bad governor as they go and he has been fair to my people, checking some abuses, but perhaps it would be a good thing to send him back to Marseilles to write an Epic! You should have seen him presiding at the Troy games at Caerleon! Farewell; and Good Fortune!

King Togidubnus

The Tacitean comment '*Britannia perdomita et statim omissa*' (*Hist.* I, 2) is a concise and memorable *sententia* but it leaves out of account the responsibility of the emperor to station troops around the frontier in the most effective way. The forces were in large part pulled back to a line between the rivers Tyne and Solway, and a military east-west road (the Stanegate) became the effective frontier. Trajan, that most military of Emperors, was happy enough with this for his expansionist aims were centred on Dacia and the East. His successor, Hadrian, had a far more interesting approach.

First the expected 'war', skirmishing, often perhaps in the aftermath of endemic cattle raiding. Then, in 122 Hadrian came to Britain. His policy for the frontier cannot be treated in isolation from his aims for the province as a whole or indeed the entire Empire. He was a thoroughgoing convert to Hellenism, and for him what made the Empire supreme amongst the peoples of the earth was its Graeco-Roman culture.

The twin eyes of the world were Athens and Rome. In Athens he completed the temple to Olympian Zeus, constructed a new quarter of the city, Hadrian's city rather than Theseus's city, with a gate at its point of entry; he built a great library, and a special cultural Senate or *Panhellenion*. At Rome the supreme monument of the

Hadrianic vision was his Pantheon replacing Agrippa's more modest building. In some ways the Chester elliptical building was its prototype. The Pantheon too was open to the sky but only at the very centre of the dome, the oculus through which the eye of Zeus could look down on the emperor seated in splendour below. The circular building recalled the ideal shape of the Oecumene, the inhabited civilised world, beyond which was the outer darkness. The empire was a commonwealth of cities.

In Britain, Hadrian would no doubt have visited some of the old cities, such as Verulamium which is conveniently near London. Whether he stayed at Chichester in the territory now, perhaps retrospectively, attributed to the *Regni*, 'the people of the kingdom', and saw the tomb of Togidubnus, who had probably died some 20 years before and was buried nearby, maybe at Hayling, we do not know; but he almost certainly went to the sanctuary at Bath and the elegant *tholos* there is ascribed to his time, and was conceivably his gift. It is likely that London was, at last, properly constituted as a city by him, for the forum is of Hadrianic date and a splendid bronze head of the emperor was dredged out of the Thames in the nineteenth century. The Cornovii of Shropshire were certainly organised as a *civitas* by Hadrian, with a town replacing the old legionary fortress at Wroxeter (*Viroconium*). The forum inscription is a proud monument to civic pride and Hadrian's prowess as builder of cities. Within the frontier, all was light; beyond the frontier was the chaos of barbaricum. The gods, so Hadrian believed, had entrusted him with the task of building a frontier wall from sea to sea for 80 miles. At Jarrow part of a war memorial begins '*Diffusis Barbaris*'; an ablative absolute, barbarians were there to be 'thoroughly scattered', but 'barbarians', as we have seen, may exist more in the mind than in actuality. Hadrian was a sane and far-sighted ruler. Hadrian's Wall was as much a symbol as the Pantheon or the Library. There was no way in which a wall could be built all the way around the Roman Empire so the shortest frontier line possible was selected. News of it would reach all corners of the great commonwealth of free cities which enjoyed Hadrian's enlightened rule.

In some ways Hadrian was the most pacific of emperors, but while the citizens enjoyed the blessings of peace, prosperity and liberty, the troops were subjected to *Discipulina*, venerated as a goddess. They were endlessly drilled, made to build forts like Hardknott, halfway up a mountain and complete with bathhouse, and then there was the Wall, bristling with watchtowers to spy out for barbarians who never came because they did not exist; though presumably anything could have menaced the civilised world from the primal chaos of the beyond: giants, amazons, griffins, harpies or great sea-serpents. More prosaically, the building activities and the garrisons kept the troops out of trouble and from the point of view of the economy they were free. Moreover such a frontier line could help to spread civilisation northwards. This it certainly did at Carlisle, perhaps at Corbridge and in the settlements which grew up outside the fort gates.

So successful was Hadrian that his successor, Antoninus, decided to repeat the whole process by moving the frontier to the Forth-Clyde line in Scotland. His excuse may have been an incursion of 'Brigantes' (perhaps peoples north of Hadrian's Wall) into the 'Gernounian district', wherever that was (Pausanias VIII, 43, 3-4). The Antonine Wall was only built of turf but the commemorative stones set up by the legionaries along its length are the one consistent programme of 'State Reliefs' in Britain. One stone shows the inevitable battle between Romans and Barbarians followed by the sacrifice to the gods; others show captives, and Roma giving a wreath to an eagle on a standard, then there are inevitably representations of Victory and of Mars. The news of Imperial victory was again disseminated by the Imperial propaganda machine, for example by means of coins. The Antonine Wall in the event proved more difficult to maintain and was abandoned by the end of the century.

Under Marcus Aurelius there was a campaign in northern Britain during the governorship of Calpurnius Agricola, c.AD 163 (*SHA, Marcus Antoninus* 8, 7), but the reason for this, whether military need or more probably serving the purposes of propaganda is uncertain. Much more interesting as a demonstration of the use of Britain in helping to regulate the Empire was the drafting of regiments of Sarmatian cavalrymen from north-eastern Europe to Britain (*SHA, Marcus Antoninus*, 22.1; Dio, *Ep.* LXXI, 16, 2) clearly to keep potentially dangerous tribesmen far from where they could cause trouble, while at the same time, civilising (Romanising) them.

Commodus, Marcus' unworthy son, was even more in need of victories other than those he won in the arena as the new Hercules, achievements which the ruling class of the Empire despised. Indeed, Ulpius Marcellus, a stern disciplinarian, was sent to Britain, clearly with the idea of keeping the troops busy (Dio, *Ep.* LXXII, 8). The story was that tribesmen had crossed the Wall, though whether this was Hadrian's Wall or, more probably, the Antonine Wall, is uncertain. The campaign at least allowed Commodus to strike medallions and coins advertising his British victories.

Britain was not however safe; disaffection came not from the northern Britons but from within the army itself, only put down when Pertinax was sent to Britain to restore order (*SHA Pertinax* 3, 5-10). Pertinax hardly made himself popular in Britain or in Rome. After Commodus was assassinated by some Praetorians in 192, Pertinax who assumed the throne was cut down a few months later. The attempt to sell the post of Emperor to the highest bidder, in the person of a senator from Milan called Didius Julianus, could hardly settle matters and a scenario developed in which Britain and other parts of the Empire could no longer be merely parking lots for legions but instead reserves of manpower ready and willing to march on the centre each spearheaded by its own candidate. The governor of Britain, Clodius Albinus, was one of the contenders. The others were Septimius Severus from Pannonia and Pescennius Niger with forces from Syria. Stategically Severus seized the advantage by supporting Albinus in Britain while he destroyed Niger. He then withdrew recognition from Albinus who crossed with his army, denuding Britain of many of its troops. At Lyons in AD 197 he defeated and killed Albinus, for the loss, we are told, of many soldiers on each side (Herodian II, 15, 1-5; III, 5 , 2-8; III, 7, 1; Dio, *Ep.* LXXV, 4-7). Not surprisingly there was some trouble in Britain, both re-establishing discipline in the army and dealing with what, all things considered, were probably only minor incursions and raids in frontier lands. The governor Virus Lupus had to buy peace or at least pay subsidies to the Meatae (Dio, *Ep.* LXXV, 5, 4).

It was clear by about 206-7 that war again threatened, but in this case the source lay in the Imperial palace in the fratricidal hatreds of Severus's sons Caracalla and Geta. It was decided that they should take part in a campaign and the field for endeavour chosen was Britain, which only 10 years before had been the power-base of Severus' rival. This would furnish victories, the more potent in that the emperor was here himself, would allow a thoroughgoing review of army discipline, and would enable Severus to show himself to the provincials. Since Hadrian the only ruling emperor seen in Britain was the usurping Albinus. The advantage of Britain was that the north had the ready expanse of mountain and moorland over which Agricola had fought before; it made an ideal 'adventure playground' for the princes.

Supply preparations in the south were extensive. New quays were built in London and as the discarded lead sealings with Imperial images on them show, important materials were unpacked here. The local economy was boosted and rich houses with splendid mosaics such as the Bucklersbury pavement date from this time. No doubt the Magnus Portus around the Solent was used. An altar from Dorcic (Dorchester in Oxfordshire) shows Marcus Varius Severus, a *beneficiarius consularis*, in charge of the local posting station, erecting an altar with screen to Jupiter. The lettering with its contractions suggests a date of around this time and activity on the roads.

For the most part, though, activity was in the north, with supply centred at South Shields and in southern Scotland at Carpow. We find the recommissioning of forts in southern Scotland or attempts to do so, for example in the sending of an *architectus* (engineer) called Amandus (RIB 2091) to Birrens. Troops may have been assembled at Newstead too where an intaglio depicting a bust of the young Caracalla has recently been found. Expectancy was in the air:

> The Virgin in the Heavens [the Empress, Julia Domna] rides on the Lion. She is the carrier of the grain, the inventor of justice, the founder of cities and through whom it is the fortune of mankind to know the gods. She is the Mother of the Gods [Cybele], Peace, Virtue, Ceres, the *Dea Syria* [Caelestis] who weighs life and law in her balance. Syria has sent this constellation to Libya [Severus came from Leptis Magna] to be venerated; this we all know. Marcus Caecilius Donatianus, tribune in the post of prefect, by the emperor's gift, has understood this led by your *numen* [divine spirit] (*RIB* 1791).

This inscription from Carvoran expresses the quasi-religious fervour of the time. The campaign was to be endowed with a mythic dimension. A gem from Castlesteads shows a bust of Severus as Zeus Sarapis flanked on either side by those of his sons as the Dioscuri. According to Herodian (III, 14, 3-10) he left Geta to look after the civil administration of the south while he and Caracalla marched north, though this statement is at odds with Herodian's earlier statement (III, 14, 2-3) that both his sons were to enjoy army discipline. The campaign was difficult because of the lack of a visible enemy. As has been suggested happened much earlier under Julius Agricola, the native tribesmen of Scotland took themselves out of harm's way.

27 *Altar set up by M. Varius Severus, a* beneficiarius consularis, *at Dorchester, Oxfordshire*

[Severus] did not fight any battles and he did not see the enemy in battle formation. Instead they deliberately left sheep and cattle in the path of the Romans for the soldiers to seize so that they might be enticed further and wear themselves out' (Dio, *Ep.* LXXVI, 13).

The war yielded its crop of victories, which continued even after Severus' death at York on 4 February 211. This was proclaimed on coins of both Severus and Caracalla and on gems handed out to supporters. A sardonyx cameo in Paris shows Severus sacrificing with his sons being crowned by victories and the legend 'To the Victory of the Emperors'. A cornelian intaglio found near Lincoln takes up the theme by figuring Caracalla as Hercules, with whom he delighted to be identified just as Commodus had done; here he is being crowned by Victory in honour of his prowess. An interesting aspect of this find, a fine example of Imperial gem-cutting, is that it seems to have been reset later in the third century in a low-quality disc brooch. There would come a time when Caracalla was best forgotten. Meanwhile

28 Bronze coin of AD 210-12 recording Severus' 'Victoria Brittanicae'

though he would be celebrated as divine: another gem, from Silchester, a green chrome chalcedony, not only shows him sacrificing in the guise of the *Genius* of the Roman people, but places the corn-measure of Sarapis on his head. In the field is a military trumpet (*tuba*) and a vexillum-head. Adulation of imperial achievements was not confined to the élite. Apart from coins scattered to the populace there were cakes portraying the Imperial family sacrificing, a mould for making them having been found at Silchester.

The regime clearly put over the message very powerfully that the Province had been restored. This is further shown by the construction, at last, of the elliptical building at Chester, evidently on the old Flavian plan though the foundations had long been covered over and lost. This time the 'Sebasteion' seems to have been completed. Hadrian's Wall was fully reconditioned and it seems that the idea grew up that the Wall had actually been built by Severus (Eutropius VIII, 19, 1; Orosius, *Adversum Paganos* VII, 17, 7-8; also Jerome, *Chronica*, AD 207, placing it in the aftermath of the Albinan revolt).

29a Chrome chalcedony from Silchester showing Caracalla as the Genius of the Roman people. He wears a corn measure on his head equating him with Sarapis. In the field a vexillum head and a long military trumpet (tuba). Height 20mm.

Herodian (III, 15, 6-7) tells us that after his father's death '[Caracalla] came to terms with the barbarians granting them peace in return for pledges of good faith'. Then he, Geta and Julia Domna hurried back to Rome with the cremated remains of Severus in an urn of purple stone either Porphyry (from Egypt) or a Fluorspar from Derbyshire known locally today as 'Blue John' (Dio, *Ep.* LXXVI, 15, 4). The ceremony of Imperial cremation and *consecratio* was impressive, and culminated in an eagle being released from the pyre to fly up to the immortal gods with the Emperor's soul. Severus had indeed entered the world of demigods and heroes in his own mind long before. Handling the urn on his deathbed he said 'You will hold a man whom the whole world could not hold'.

Histories of Roman Britain focus on the military events between Claudius and Severus. On the ground, archaeology deals with the ditches and walls of forts and apparently all the paraphernalia of conquest. The Romans are often portrayed as practical; in fact they lived far more in a world of ideas, codifying the world in terms

29b Dark cornelian intaglio found near Lincoln but reset later in the third century in a cheap bronze brooch. It shows Victory crowning Caracalla, shown here as Hercules. Height 19mm. Photo: Institute of Archaeology, Oxford

of personification and metaphor. The Roman State developed the visual imagery of Hellenism, refining it to a series of symbols. Being a Roman officer demanded the capacity of being open to extraordinary visions of gods leading heroic armies and imagining oneself on the plains of Marathon or Gaugamela as a representative of the forces of civilisation facing the ever-waiting barbarian.

It is time to turn again to the south, and to observe similar leaps of the imagination at work amongst the youth of Roman Britain as they entered with zest into the cultural inheritance of the commonwealth of the Empire. In this at least, the passion of the 'sons of chiefs' for the liberal arts, Tacitus' *topos* (in *Agricola* 21) would appear to have been nothing but the truth.

Primus turned to Strato. He had an idea. 'Soldiers arm themselves against the barbarians just as we arm ourselves against demons! I visited one of my father's farms and his bailiff was dedicating an altar to Mars and the god is shown as a soldier with spear and shield.'

'That is true', said Strato, 'for us Greeks too. Warrior gods and heroes protect us, and always have! You can think of gods and men being assailed by myriad demons and we have to campaign against them just as Achilles did, or Tacitus' relative Agricola.'

'I can magic them away, said Primus. Lucius told me all you have to do is to write:

ROTAS
OPERA
TENET
AREPO
SATOR

One above the other just like that!'

Strato affected to be surprised. 'What do those words mean: "The sower Arepo holds the wheels that turn".'

Primus sounded superior. 'They are SPECIAL words. Read them right to left, left to right, top to bottom and bottom to top. They are magic. Lucius scratched them on his bedroom wall . . . his mother was not best pleased but he said it kept the demons away!'

'What you have found', said Strato, 'is the power of words, the power of individual letters and their virtues. Euphonious sounds, names of power like that of the god Iao or Iao Sabaoth from the Hebrew, or Chnoubis from the Egyptian, even the chanting of alphabets to keep off malignant forces like Typhon who inhibits childbirth. Of course images on gemstones of Iao, Isis or combinations of human and animal forms are also thought by some to help in this battle. It may be that they do, but the best specific in our battles against the Evil Eye is in gathering knowledge. So my young hero, here are two charms for you, a sword, by which I mean your iron stylus and a shield, your waxed tablet.'

'Can I have a plan of campaign?', Primus laughed, entering into the joke.

'Shall we rise through the air and fight dragons?', said Strato.

'Yes please!' Primus replied.

'We will start, then, with the *Metamorphoses* and you will see where we came from and where we are going to.'

'Is it as "true" as what the army did in Britain?' Primus enquired.

'Truer', answered Strato. 'You will, I hope, in due course be garlanded by Victory, as a worthy son of Rome. You will strike down ignorance and come away the victor!'

4 Paedeia: the making of a gentleman

Primus was growing tired. 'What has all this old Latin poetry which we are going through letter by letter and word by word got to do with life in modern Corinium?'

Strato sympathised with his restlessness. 'Perhaps I can explain. Let us take a walk through the city and look at some statues and a few pictures . . . First what is that great column with the statue on top?'

'That', said Primus with a proprietorial air, 'is our great column of Jupiter. My grand-father gave it to the town, as a thank you for getting a big contract to ship a lot of pots up north for the army. Jupiter, you know, is not just a Roman god, and not just your Greek Zeus. He is our sky god too. We Celts sometimes call him Tanaris.'

'But who are those figures peering out of the leaves, around the capital?'

Primus looked uncertain. 'I suppose, Strato', he said, 'they are powers of nature who support his majesty.'

'Indeed they are! The first one with grapes in his hair and a wand, a thyrsus, behind his left shoulder, that is his son by Semele, none other than the wine-god Bacchus. Semele wanted to see her husband as he really was, and Zeus could not deny her. She was burnt to ashes but the son . . . Bacchus was saved. Next to him is Bacchus' lady love Ariadne, daughter of King Minos of Crete. You remember those lovely lines in Ovid's *Metamorphoses* after Theseus had abandoned her on Naxos: "Ariadne, abandoned, was bewailing her fate when Bacchus threw his arms around her and rescued her, taking her diadem from her head and putting it in the heavens for a constellation for her everlasting glory". Then we can see a jolly Silenus with his knobbly vine staff and a drinking cup, a rhyton full of good cheer; and finally a woolly barbarian. That is Lycurgus, king of the Thracian Edones who tried to kill the nymph Ambrosia with his axe, and was himself strangled by Ambrosia whom Bacchus had turned into a vine. You could interpret them as the four seasons, spring, summer, autumn and winter, I suppose.'

Primus's eyes opened wider. 'I know. It is just like the mosaic pavement we have at home. Mother says it is one of the nicest in Corinium. It has a wonderful Silenus on a donkey too . . . and a really nasty scene. A man turning into a stag, like our Celtic Cernunnos, only this isn't a god; he is a man being torn to pieces by hounds! It's horrid!'

'That poor man', said Strato, 'is called Actaeon and again we can find the story in Ovid. By accident he saw Diana bathing, something no mortal should do, so she punished him with death. These stories are Greek stories too. When you grow up wherever you wander in the Empire you can share all of these tales with the important people you meet . . . and tell them one or two of your Celtic tales as well.'

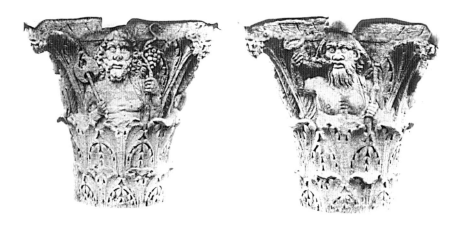

30 *Capital of Jupiter Column, Cirencester (shown are two faces, Lycurgus with vine, and Silenus). Height 1.06m.* Institute of Archaeology, Oxford, Archive

What did the Roman Britons read?

One of Tacitus' *topoi* was that the sons of chieftains were trained in rhetoric and excelled at the bar. There is no need to doubt this for such training defined *Romanitas*. Although no volumes of insular prose writing survive until the late Empire with Patrick and Faustus of Riez in the fifth century and Gildas in the sixth, it is probable that such stylists as Cicero and Quintilian whose influence has been traced in these early Christian writers, would have been studied at school from quite early on.

The poetry of Vergil and Ovid were likewise widely known and left their mark in quotations of the former and adaptations of the latter while the popularity of works of art with mythological scenes is best explained, in many instances, by the popularity and influence of the *Metamorphoses*. For instance amongst second-century floors are the Actaeon mosaic at Corinium drawing on book three and a mosaic from Leicester showing Cyparissus with his pet stag from book ten. No doubt there were British poets throughout Roman times, but the only one recorded as having published his work is the fourth-century Silvius Bonus, the butt of Ausonius' wit in his *Epigrams* (107-12) which he probably released in 382. 'Bonus could not possibly be a good poet because no Britain could be a good poet.' Nevertheless verse found occasionally on tombstones and on mosaics such as the couplet from the Lullingstone triclinium packs in elegance and erudition (see below), while the contrast between the realms of Bacchus and Neptune in the lines surrounding the largest room at Frampton appears equally polished and erudite.

Sidonius Apollinaris in fifth-century Gaul provides evidence for the reading of much else even at an elementary level, from the poet Statius to the plays of Terence and the histories of Sallust. Furthermore Greek was studied, notably Homer and the plays of Menander. No doubt education in the major centres of Britain was always just as comprehensive, even though evidence is sadly lacking.

*31 Maker's name
Tamesubugus
from mortaria
made near
Oxford*

TA·Mιι·ſυ.Bν.Gνſ·Fι∖

Mιι·Sν·Bν·Gνς·fιι·cιτ·

At its simplest level literacy is expressed by writing exercises on tiles (subsequently fired) or scratched alphabets on potsherds. Even quite humble people such as potters were able to produce attractive cursive signatures, like Tamesubugus of the Oxfordshire (Headington) pottery. A higher standard of latinity was unavoidable among the ruling classes of the towns and country villas. No school-site has been recognised by archaeologists, not surprisingly as the only diagnostic feature to be expected would be iron styli and waxed wooden tablets, and maybe the remains of an abacus, used for counting and simple arithmetic. A rubbish dump at Vindolanda has, however, yielded a line from book ix of the *Aeneid* (ix, 473), '*Interea pavidam volitans pinna[ta per urbem]*': 'Meanwhile, winged Fame, flitting through the trembling town . . .' It is written in capitals probably by the son of the commander, a Batavian aristocrat called Cerealis. The *grammaticus* seems to have added the comment 'sloppy work' to the exercise, so it was not just the town that was trembling! Discipline was tough in a Roman school.

Doubtless his contemporaries in the southern British cities could do as well – or as badly. A tile from Silchester contains a graffito in a practised cursive hand, including the opening words of *Aeneid* ii, Conticuere omnes; 'All fell silent' (*RIB* 2491. 148); this too is probably a writing exercise. Public teaching of such elementary subjects would have been given by a *grammaticus* and lessons often took place in the forum (where I have set Primus' lessons from Strato). The wealthy landowners in the countryside would have provided such instruction in their villas. A funerary relief from Neumagen in the Moselle valley shows a teacher and two pupils seated reading from scrolls; a third pupil has arrived late, bearing his sachel and has raised his hand to make excuses. The learning of lines of poetry by heart was designed to make the treasures of Latin literature familiar to the pupil; later at a level beyond that mechanical skill came composition, enabling him to impress his friends and equals. Perhaps it is not very surprising that the children of the upper classes, often with private tutors as shown on the school-scene relief just mentioned, were able to do what so many schoolboys down to very recently did without too much difficulty, compose Latin verse or intersperse formal speeches with an epigram. It is likely that girls would often have shared in this primary education. The mother of the poet Ausonius in fourth-century Gaul went to school with the boys and like them was flogged for misdemeanours. However women did not normally enter on the much more demanding studies of philosophy, higher mathematics and declamation which a *rhetor* would provide once a boy had reached the age of 16 or so.

32 A school scene; relief from Neumagen near Trier. Photo: Professor Anthony King

It would seem that schoolboys in Roman Britain employed tricks to aid memory including mnemonics. One item of evidence here comes from an unlikely source, numismatics. In the late third century the Emperor Carausius put out coins to appeal to the local Roman patriotism of well-to-do provincials. An intriguing group of coins has the mintmark RSR while a medallion has the additional letters I.N.P.C.D.A. Together these letters are the initial ones of two lines of Vergil's fourth Eclogue (6-7) – *Redeunt Saturnia Regna, Iam Nova Progenies Caelo Demittitur Alto*, 'The Age of Saturn returns; now a new generation is sent down from high heaven'. In itself such use of initials was familiar; tombstones for example bore the letters DM for 'Dis Manibus'. Here however fairly oblique coin legends were designed to carry high political charges. Other Carausian coins hail the Emperor as 'the long-awaited one', *Expectate Veni*, which is a tag from *Aeneid* ii, 283, perhaps rather inappropriate as it is concerned with Hector's ghost. Plenty is evoked in the coin legend *Ubertas*, and the image of a girl milking a cow brings to mind passages in the Eclogues (iii.30; iv.22) and Georgics (ii.524). Of course, these coins were not designed for the use of intellectuals – intellectuals never have any money; they reflect the same average understanding that some of the better-known passages of Shakespeare do with us, 'To be or not to be, that is the question' etc.

Alongside them was the excitement known to every schoolchild in creating puzzles and breaking cyphers. A series of five words scratched on an interior wall of Corinium (*RIB* 2447.20): *Rotas/Opera/Tenet/Arepo/Sator* is a palindrome known throughout the Empire. The words can be read in any direction; they have a near mystical meaning – 'The sower Arepo holds the wheels which turn' – and the letters can be rearranged to read 'Pater noster' with two letter as and two letter os left over, standing for the Greek letters Alpha and Omega. Despite appearances the square appears to be pre-Christian in origin. In the fourth century, counting and mystical interpretation became more widespread; both seem to be present in the two line

33a Reverse of coin with Vergilian phrase,   *33b Medallion with I.N.P.C.D.A.*
  'Expectate veni' and RSR 'mintmark'   *'mintmark', together the letters*
                          RSRINPCDA recall the theme of the
                          Fourth Eclogue.
                          Drawings by Guy de la Bédoyère

verse of one of the most famous mosaic floors in Britain, that at Lullingstone, Kent.
Here, using an Ovidian metre and the Ovidian story of Europa and the Bull, the villa
owner alludes to the storm from book ii of the *Aeneid*, that wrecked the Trojan fleet.
He also encodes his name Avitus together with the name of Jesus, thus showing
himself to be a Christian. Such encoding should be looked for elsewhere. One possibility is of course that lines on another mosaic, at Frampton in Dorset, should be read
as a cryptogram although, so far, all attempts to count, numerate or rearrange letters
here have been unsuccessful. Nevertheless, even so, there is an allusive meaning to be
found here. Neptune is shown frequently in art as for instance in the centre of a
second-century mosaic at Verulamium. Often, as on the mosaic at Frampton or upon
the great silver dish from Mildenhall in Suffolk, his realm seems to be contrasted with
that of Bacchus who, at Frampton, is symbolised by Cupid, the type of the infant
Bacchus, as well as by two other representations of the god. It looks from the iconography as though the owner of the complex was concerned with some sort of private
cult. He was clearly educated, and a lover of literary themes, again drawn from the
Metamorphoses, including scenes showing Aeneas plucking the golden bough,
Cadmus spearing the serpent of Mars, and probably Perseus striking the sea-monster
(though as he is provided with a trident rather than his usual two-pronged sword, or
harpe, he might be Neptune).

Evidence that the rich imagery of figured mosaic often takes us back to what had
been learned in the schoolroom is also provided by a mythological mosaic from the
great western chamber of the palatial villa at Keynsham, Somerset. Out of what were
originally six mythological scenes, three remain. One scene probably shows the myth

of Achilles being sheltered, disguised as a girl amongst the daughters of King Lycomedes and being discovered by Ulysses and Diomedes, the source here being perhaps Statius' *Achilleid* or the *Genealogiae* of the second-century writer, Hyginus, popular in school use. Then we see Europa and the bull, a more placid version than at Lullingstone and evidently depicting the moment before the bull takes off, but probably drawn from Ovid and, finally, a story popular with Ovid (given at length in the *Fasti* and mentioned in the *Metamorphoses*) but also found in Hyginus, that of Minerva inventing the *tibiae*; she was disgusted by the reflection of her face puffed up through playing them when she looked at her reflection in the water and threw them away. They were recovered by the satyr Marsyas with direful consequences for himself.

Probably even more significant than Ovid, Hyginus or Statius in Roman education was Vergil, especially his masterpiece the *Aeneid*. The famous Vergilian pavement from Low Ham, likewise in Somerset, tells the story of Dido and Aeneas, from the arrival of the Trojans at Carthage, after the storm at sea to which the Lullingstone couplet mentioned above, also alludes. We see their reception by Dido, the royal hunt and the lovemaking of Dido and Aeneas. The cruel but inevitable separation of the pair, driven apart by Aeneas' sense of duty, is prefigured by the hero remaining in armour while Dido is naked. Finally Dido's suicide is shown figuratively by one of the cupids beside Venus holding her torch down while the other holds it up to represent Aeneas' ultimate triumph. All the scenes are similarly spare in their arrangement and highly allusive in their storytelling. Their power comes from knowing books ii and iv of the *Aeneid* by heart and from loving them. Even the young Augustine of Hippo wept for Dido and so it seems did the children of Roman Britain. Clearly there were also Vergilian wall paintings. A piece of wall plaster from the villa at Otford, Kent bears in neat capitals the two words 'BINA MANV L . . .'(*RIB* 2447.9), part of the line '*bina manu lato crispans hastilia ferro*' meaning 'grasping in his hand two shafts tipped with broad steel', which may refer to Aeneas exploring the land of Carthage (*Aeneid* i, 313) and the same well-loved episodes of the early part of the poem though the line recurs in xii, 165, dealing with Turnus advancing to fight Aeneas. Fragments of figures, one holding a spear, suggest ambitious figural work. One remarkable piece of evidence which emphasises the likely presence of classical learning at the highest level is the codex, now in the Vatican, known as the *Vergilius Romanus*. Here a text of the poet is accompanied by illustrations in a terse, linear style, certainly west European and almost certainly Romano-British. The illustrations are not directly related to Low Ham, though they point to the near certainty that the proprietor of the Low Ham villa owned a similar manuscript. Sidonius Apollinaris informs us that in fifth-century Gaul, rich landowners like Tonantius Ferreolus at Prusianum had extensive private libraries of the Classics (and in that Christian milieu, devotional works). The same was surely true of Britain in the fourth century, and even later. The survival of the Vatican codex is fortuitous; interestingly it was in France in the Middle Ages, and we can speculate whether it was preserved in Western Britain, or in Ireland (as some believe), during the so-called Dark Ages. As the writing of Gildas shows us together with the relatively numerous fifth century and later inscribed stones of Wales and Dumnonia, literacy certainly did not die out and Roman style schooling was maintained at famous monastic sites such as St Illtyd's school at Llantwit Major (Llanilltud Fawr) in Glamorgan, where literacy and games with letters were taught in the time honoured way, albeit now with a strong Christian basis.

There are other examples of figural mosaic which arise not from casual whim but from cultural conditioning. For example, the popularity of Bellerophon, who appears on no less than four fourth-century mosaics from Britain, cannot originate from the copybook of a mosaic workshop which just *happened* to have this particular scene in its repertoire. The owner would have specifically asked for the device because it meant something to him, presumably symbolic of the victory of good over evil. The source here may well have been the *Genealogiae* of Hyginus but the local cultural gloss may have been Christian exegesis, because in three instances (Lullingstone, Frampton and Hinton St Mary) the mosaics include Christian elements.

Even more striking as an instance of special selection of a theme in Britain is Orpheus and the beasts. He is shown on a number of distinctive mosaics of a type which first appears in Cirencester during the early fourth century, and differs from that prevalent in the rest of the Empire in that the British Orpheus is shown alone with his hound or fox in the centre, while animals and birds radiate around him in concentric registers rather than in the centre of a rectangular panel with the beasts packed in with him. Clearly classical literary sources were used, though probably something more recondite than the brief reference in Ovid to the animals congregating around him at the beginning of book xi of the *Metamorphoses*, especially as the passage is immediately followed by his death at the hands of the Ciconian women. Esoteric neo-Platonic and Orphic sources, deriving from higher, University-type learning and philosophical speculation must be involved: here everything is in motion around the still, untroubled centre of the world, and we are in the same world as philosophers like Plotinus who by theurgy, trance-like states, could raise themselves to the highest heavens. A philosopher or pagan holy-man, with sundial, globe and staff appears (as we will see) in the centre of the main floor of the villa at Brading on the Isle of Wight where, incidentally, a figure of Orpheus is shown on a mosaic at what may be the threshold of the house.

There was, however, a local element to the Orpheus of Corinium as well. Despite a tendency for scholars to write about the Britons as though they were merely passive recipients of culture, this is very far from being the case. From early times the Celts were great and inventive storytellers, and when the Celtic languages came to be written down late in the Middle Ages they gave rise, for example, to the Welsh *Mabinogion* and the Irish *Tain* – though of course by then these were much influenced by outside sources. The Cirencester Dobunni seem to have had no difficulty conflating Graeco-Roman Orpheus with their own local hunter god, Apollo Cunomaglos, Apollo the 'hound-prince'. Primus would have been able to point to any number of images. The hound-prince and Orpheus were combined as powerful beings, demigods or gods, who could control nature. It is possible that something of Attis was combined with this composite figure. No doubt he was celebrated (under what name we do not know) in hymns and epic verse.

34a The Cotswold hunter god as he appears at Chedworth, Gloucestershire, height 45.5cm

Such a combination of the deeply classical and the Celtic is actually provable in the case of Faunus, an obscure god from Latium (the countryside around Rome), only known to us because he appears in poets such as Vergil, Ovid and Horace. It was clearly this poetry which was brought to Britain, not the Italian cult. The evidence comes from a late Roman treasure of silver and jewellery from Thetford, Norfolk. Here some of the spoons are inscribed with legends such as '*Dei Fauni Auseci*' (prick-eared) or '*Dei Fauni Nari*' (noble, great-hearted); or '*Dei Fauni Crani*' (god of hoards) or '*Dei Fauni Medugeni*' (the 'mead-begotten'). These are Celtic epithets and the character of the god, noble, giver of drink and treasure is a constant in Celtic society. Nevertheless, Classical sophistication is shown by spoons bearing the names (cult *signa* rather than personal names) of votaries such as Ingenuus, Primigenia, Silviola and Perseveria meaning native-born, first-born, she of the woodlands, she who has persevered. Other allusion is iconographic. One gold ring has a bezel in the form of a human head with rather goat like features and horns, recognisable as those of Faunus or Pan; another, more subtly, is embellished with a wine cup and has a pair of woodpeckers (Latin name *picus*) as supporters in allusion to Picus, Faunus' father. Faunus himself is figured on a gold buckle in the form of a satyr and the cult, like so many late Roman cults gravitated towards that of the wine god, the saviour god Bacchus. A silver gilt spoon portrays a bounding feline; another evokes the marine thiasos with a triton. Both have legends hailing the god as '*Dei Nari*'.

We lack the hymns of praise, such as we know were sung by choirs at Ephesus for Artemis and at Claros for Apollo, and at other sanctuaries in the Greek world. But we may have the arenas in which they were sung. The greatest meeting centres outside the cities were the ovoid or circular amphitheatres. In the Roman coloniae such as Colchester and certainly at London these would have been largely for beast fights and gladiatorial displays; while at the military fortresses they were centres for weapon-training but these activities did not ever really become very popular in Britain. We can tell that by the lack of interest in the works of art commissioned by the gentry. Throughout their existence these arenas must have been difficult to maintain and were sometimes prone to flood. But they were ideal meeting places for a populace and the strange local pots made for sale at fairs in Eastern Britain could point to their uses as fairgrounds. But an obvious use was for the singing competitions known in Welsh as *Eisteddfods*. The very narrow

34b Detail of Orpheus from mosaic at Littlecote, Wiltshire

amphitheatre at Carmarthen would have been fairly useless for shows of the normal Roman kind. A circular amphitheatre at Frilford in Oxfordshire is closely connected with a temple and would presumably have been the centre of ceremonies connected with the deity venerated here, while at Verulamium the theatre-amphitheatre was associated not just with a temple but with a sacred way stretching up the hill to the Folly Lane sanctuary.

We can, perhaps, sense the mixture of local continuity and Graeco-Roman erudition at a sanctuary by taking the case of Lydney on the edge of the Forest of Dean, over-looking the Severn in Gloucestershire. The god here was called Nodens, and the name has been thought cognate with the Irish Nuada 'of the silver hand'. Celtic specialists often discuss the cult as though this can be done in largely Celtic terms; there is a contrary tendency of Classicists (including formerly myself) to rather discount the native element, at least insofar as the more sophisticated worshippers were concerned. What about the man who laid the mosaic in the second half of the fourth century? Titus Flavius Senilis was proud of his *tria nomina* long after people in parts of the Empire nearer the centre had discarded theirs. No doubt it was part of his pagan identity as was his title, *praepositus religionum*, master of the religious rites. These rites included incubation, that is sleeping in the temple or in a long building, a 'place apart' (the Greek word *abaton* is apt), and then visiting the dream interpreter, at Lydney called Victorinus. The sacred hounds which roamed the sanctuary and licked the sores of votaries afflicted with disease could have come from Greek Epidaurus where hounds certainly performed this function.

Yet Nodens was local. He seems to have been equated with Mars (in this region an agricultural not a military deity) and the local people who came to the temple like Pectillus (*RIB* 307) were probably quite unaware of the exotic side of his cult. It belonged in the countryside just as much as did the cults of Apollo Cunomaglus at Nettleton or Mercury at Uley across the River Severn.

35   *Gilt bronze head of Sulis Minerva, from Bath. Height 25cm*

And what about Bath? Togidubnus' great monument is a tribute to his erudition, his faith in the future of the Empire and also to his people's part in it. The political resonance of its iconography might be apparent to the sophisticated, though most visitors were only struck by the wonders of the site. Solinus, for example, was fascinated by the burning of Forest of Dean coal on the eternally flaming fire in Sulis' temple producing a clinker rather than ash (*Collectanea Rerum Memorabilium* 22, 10); this was a novelty to him. Others had visions of the goddess (*RIB* 153). But many, many votaries addressed letters to Sulis inscribed on lead tablets in Latin of varying quality: some were literate scribes; other plaintiffs had difficulty transcribing texts others had laid before them. For some visitors this was Minerva in her local guise of Sulis, the same as the protective Athena of Athens, virgin child of Jupiter (Zeus); for others a local spring-goddess who could get their property back. Yet even for the local peasants there would be tales of her power to be recounted in epic or acted in the theatre by the sanctuary. In either case, the love of declamation, the desire to sing the praises of the most high gods would be powerful factors in civilisation, factors which would be carried over into Christianity whenever that faith took hold. For example a silver vessel from Water Newton bears a hexameter in the name of the dedicator, one Publianus. After an Alpha, a chi-rho and an omega it reads:

> *Sanctum altare tuum, Domine, subnixus honoro*
> 'Prostrating myself, O Lord, I honour your sacred altar' (*RIB* 2414.2).

St Patrick's *Confessio* written in the early fifth century is full of verbal tricks dating back to the beginnings of Roman oratory, including the oldest. If one wants to persuade, begin by belittling yourself: '*Ego, Patricius, peccator rusticissimus et minimus omnium fidelium et contemptibilissimus apud plurimos*' – 'I, Patrick, a sinner, totally uncultivated and the least of all the faithful and utterly despicable to many . . .'

*36 Mercury from the Bath Gate,
     Cirencester. Height 42cm.
     Photo: the late T.F.C. Blagg*

*37 Intaglio from North Cerney depicting
     countryman visiting a rustic shrine,
     perhaps of Priapus. Length 10mm.
     Photo: Institute of Archaeology,
     Oxford*

There was nothing wrong with Patrick's education as we see in the verbal dexterity of his language; what is incredible is that anyone has ever taken such statements at their face value.

Primus and Strato walked on; they admired the figures of the gods carved on the Bath gate, Mercury in his floppy hat and Minerva with her breastplate bearing the gorgon mask. It seemed that everywhere was full of the gods, beautiful and ageless. Just outside the gate they met Castus, Primus' friend and contemporary who had clearly been taking the morning off, fishing. Strato could see that his charge had had enough of high culture when the two boys rushed off and started reading some graffiti scrawled on a wall of a property falling into neglect. Strato sighed, the economic situation could be better. Indeed his pay was in coin which hardly looked silver. 'Flavius is a catamite'; 'Felix is a bugger'; 'Civilis is constipated' read Primus (Strato mused 'well, at least the lad can read') and there were obscene drawings too. Strato stood patiently by . . . the boys rushed back. 'What is a "mentula"?', asked Castus, and both collapsed giggling.

38 *Phallus ('mentula')
pulling a cart, from
Wroxeter.* Institute
of Archaeology,
Oxford, archive
photo, courtesy
the late Graham
Webster

Strato with the gifts of a teacher, and great wisdom in his mind, thought for a bit. 'I was talking to you, Primus, about the gods. One of the oldest of the gods is Priapus . . . don't mock him; he is known for his wisdom, his humour . . . and his great prick . . . that is the meaning of "mentula". You are not going to escape from your lesson in culture that easily. With that Strato recited slowly, as though from memory, the lines:

*Tu, quicunque vides circa tectoria nostra
non nimium casti carmina plena ioci,
versibus obscenis offendi desine: non est
mentula subducti nostra supercilii.*

'It comes from a little volume of *Priapea* and was written 200 years ago in honour of the god. In the poem Priapus says that you will find obscene poems on the walls, but read them with joy. His prick is not quick to prudely take offence. Imagine Priapus raising his eyebrows in disapproval! Primus and Castus, we can always learn more . . . Priapus is often shown on paintings in front of our houses. You have surely seen him there? And there are figurines of him in house shrines. Why? Because he brings prosperity and protects us all from the Evil Eye.

'Laugh by all means, he likes that; but there is nothing of impurity about him. Our culture can include him and the great gods of Mount Olympus. In my country there was once a man called Alcibiades, the greatest general we ever had. He would have led us to victory in Sicily only he was arrogant and mean-spirited. In a drunken orgy, the night before he was due to sail, he and his friends cut off the "pricks" from the herms . . . don't laugh – it was sacrilege in the highest degree. The gods clearly blamed the city. Alcibiades did not sail . . . and we lost the war. When you see a phallus drawing a cart, or flying or sitting on a wall, smile by all means and "raise your eyebrows" but honour the god and make an offering to him.'

5 Politics and culture

Extracts from the archives of the city of Verulamium:

Letter of Epaticcus to the Senate and People of Rome, AD 43.
'This city, the capital of the western Catuvellauni, remains loyal to its treaty with Rome. Others of my family run riot. We, with our allies to the west the Dobunni, are beset by enemies and ask the help of Caesar. I set my seal of the Centaur holding an olive branch to this request.'

Deposition of the City treasurer, Marcus Lupus, AD 61.
'I barely escaped with my life but I rescued a handful of the archives, including the charter of Claudius honouring ancient Verulanion with the proud title of Municipium. The city is burnt; it will rise again . . . but the horror of the deaths and the looting at the hands of that savage woman Boudica will never be forgotten here. May our children never forget the perfidy of the barbarians.'

From the speech of Tiberius Claudius Togidubnus, Great King of Britain to the most noble *ordo* of Verulamium on the inauguration of the new Civic Centre. 12 February AD 79.
'Most revered councillors, I came with the governor to honour this victorious city, the *civitas* of Verulamium, which has risen phoenix-like from the ashes and now has a splendid forum. You and I are Britons with a love for this island which will live for ever; we are also citizens of Rome. Being a Roman does not mean living in Italy; I enjoyed my youth in the great city, certainly. It was exciting to be able to talk with men and women from all over the world. But our Rome is here. In you I see the future. I have a job as king; a job I must do for Rome. But the future is with you. The freedom of Britain does not lie in her kings, but in her citizens; in her fora and basilicas and above all in her schools.

'We, of the Atrebates, are ancient allies of the western Catuvellauni as of the Dobunni beyond you. This great land, tried by war, remains and ever will remain unconquered as long as there are citizens prepared to maintain its traditions.'

From the speech of Hadrian, Emperor of Rome. 3 April AD 122.
'Beloved fellow countrymen of this commonwealth of cities which stretch from here to Asia, I dedicate your new enlarged Forum with pleasure. In 40 years your city has grown in extent and wealth. I heard some of your youth sing a hymn in my honour. The sentiments made me blush behind my beard (polite laughter) . . .

but the diction was faultless. Education is our great weapon against the enemies who menace us, ignorance, bad manners and intolerance. Read our great Cicero and maybe a few of you who have mastered Latin so well will also study and enjoy Greek as well . . .'

Culture did not develop in a vacuum. The adoption of all the trappings of Roman life in first-century Britain, accompanied by the usual apparatus of self government, the forum, basilica, *ordo* and magistrates (duoviri and aediles) did not relegate those at the head of provincial society within the island to a state of passivity or amnesia. It could hardly do so when the province contained three legions composed of men who were, likewise, Roman citizens and where news about Rome and the Empire could arrive quickly.

The new province was established during a period when the majority of tribal leaders in central and southern Britain regarded themselves first as Claudian and then as Flavian clients. They were as horrified as the Roman government, when the dissident Iceni and Trinovantes rose in revolt in AD 60 in an insurrection which rejected the very concept of *Romanitas*. They had more to lose as is shown by the fate of Verulamium. The revolt could have been worse still as there is a slight hint that some of the peoples in the far south-west, specifically the Dumnonii and some of the Durotriges, were also untrustworthy; the main evidence here was the reluctance of Poenius Postumus, the camp commandant of Legio II Augusta, to move the second legion from its base in Exeter. Possible wider trouble was, indeed, threatened even after the revolt was put down by the insensitive behaviour of the governor Suetonius Paullinus, who in seeking retribution may not have been too rigorous in distinguishing between friend and foe. Here the procurator Fabius Alpinus Classicianus who probably came, like his wife Julia Pacata Indiana, from the highest echelons of Gaulish society put a stop to such reprisals, perhaps (though we are not told so) in concert with King Togidubnus. His interference is not kindly treated by Tacitus but quite clearly reconciliation was the only way of establishing peace with the defeated tribes.

While the legions in Britain were inevitably drawn into the faction fighting around the vacancy for the principate in the years AD 68-70, following Vindex's revolt in Gaul and Nero's precipitate suicide, this hardly concerned the civilians to any extent, though it is possible that King Togidubnus gained enhanced favour with the faction which eventually prevailed by backing Vespasian, perhaps an old friend from the events of AD 43. The Flavian period saw the increasing spread of Romanisation, epitomised by the inscription dedicating the Forum of Verulamium in AD 79 during the governorship of Agricola. The Emperor at the time was Titus who seems to have been very popular in Britain. Suetonius tells us that his statues were everywhere; his source here was probably Tacitus. Although many of these statues will have been set up as part of the Flavian building programme, it is very possible that Togidubnus (a near contemporary) might have been an enthusiastic dedicator of such images.

39 Denarius of Clodius Albinus.
Photo: Institute of
Archaeology, Oxford

Throughout the period spanning the end of the first and most of the second century the economy boomed, stimulated in 122, no doubt, by the visit of the Emperor Hadrian who was interested in seeing local aristocracies develop. As he had been born in Italica in Spain he had a large degree of sympathy with the upper classes of other provinces though, no doubt, the more Greek-style the culture he encountered, the more pleased he would have been. The Antonine age is the time in which substantial town houses were constructed in such towns as Verulamium, which certainly had municipal status, and Cirencester and Leicester which probably did. These *domus* were embellished with wall paintings and mosaics, laid by flourishing local workshops, and the countryside around them was increasingly Romanised, with substantial villas appearing throughout southern Britain. Inscriptions – building dedications, statue bases, altars and tombstones – would have celebrated both individual and corporate achievement. There was no reason why the owner of an estate or a successful merchant should, in any way, oppose the rule of an Empire of which he was a stakeholder and beneficiary.

The first problem really came as a result of Commodus's assassination. The antics of an unworthy emperor did not in themselves upset far-away Britain, where the system of Imperial government continued to run smoothly, but an emperor's death without heirs inevitably led to a power struggle as in 68-9, although with the difference that in this case one of the candidates was the governor of Britain, Clodius Albinus. Inevitably the effects of patronage, friendship and alliance with a man who would, it was hoped, rule the entire Roman world brought the leaders of the Britons directly into Imperial politics. An immediate advantage was, it seems, the grant of permission to build town walls. The possession of fortifications was seen as much as a sign of status as of defense. Other favours were doubtless promised and had Albinus defeated his main rival

Septimius Severus at Lyons in 197 it is quite likely that Britons would have entered the Senate and eventually achieved governorships in some numbers.

Instead, the advent of Septimius Severus was, at first, a definite setback. A soldier from Leptis Magna with a Syrian wife, Severus favoured his own protegés, many of them easterners. Doubtless Britain saw rough justice meted out by Imperial agents, which cannot have been helpful. A minor consideration behind the Severan visit to Britain in 208 may have been to root out those who remained hostile to the regime, even if the main reason was to toughen up the emperor's sons in campaigning in the Scottish mountains. An Imperial adventus, however, inevitably had some beneficial effects on civilian life (at least on those civilians never involved with Albinus), stimulating as it did commercial activity and certainly in London, the capital, a number of very fine mosaics date from the time, including the Bucklersbury pavement, technically one of the finest geometric floors from the province. How popular were the Severans in civilian circles? In Silchester, certainly, they were eating cakes stamped with scenes celebrating the Imperial victories and someone lost a fine engraved chrome-chalcedony gemstone, a handsome green-coloured signet, showing Caracalla as the *Genius* of the Roman People. Other communities also prospered, notably York in the north of the civilian zone, where a Colonia was founded. The settlement lying on the opposite bank of the Ouse from the fortress of Legio VI would have had a population in which veterans and their families dominated the social scene, making it an ideal candidate for such enhanced status. Indeed, York became a provincial capital for Severus divided the province into two, the South ruled from London being known as Britannia Superior and the north, centred on York, Britannia Inferior. The former was symbolised on provincial seals by a bull; Southern Britain by a stag. The stag, which is shown on one sealing from London, crouching at the feet of Britannia, *Britannia Sancta* (Holy Britannia) as the legend says (*RIB* 2411.33), may have been chosen because it was associated with the ever-popular hunter god of Southern Britain; the bull was simply the device of Legio VI, based at York.

Caracalla, anxious to widen the tax base, issued an edict early in his reign (AD 212) giving citizenship to all free inhabitants of the Empire. In fact this privilege did not bestow equality on all and sundry, for there was a superior upper class (the *honestiores*, the 'most honest', the richer citizens) and a much larger group below them (the *humiliores* or more humble, poorer citizens). However, direct evidence for the political and civic life of either class is hard to find in the province during this period. Much more momentous was Caracalla's introduction of a double denarius which nevertheless only contained the amount of silver to be expected in one and a half denarii. This was the start of an inflation in which Britain could not but share alongside the other economic problems of the rest of the Empire. Nevertheless the increasingly debased coinage of the century become ubiquitous as site finds, appearing in remote places where coins were not found previously, and so attesting a slight advance in one aspect of Romanisation. For example a little farm within an old Iron Age hillfort at Alfred's Castle, Oxfordshire has yielded a couple of dozen coins for the second half of the third century and early fourth century. There is

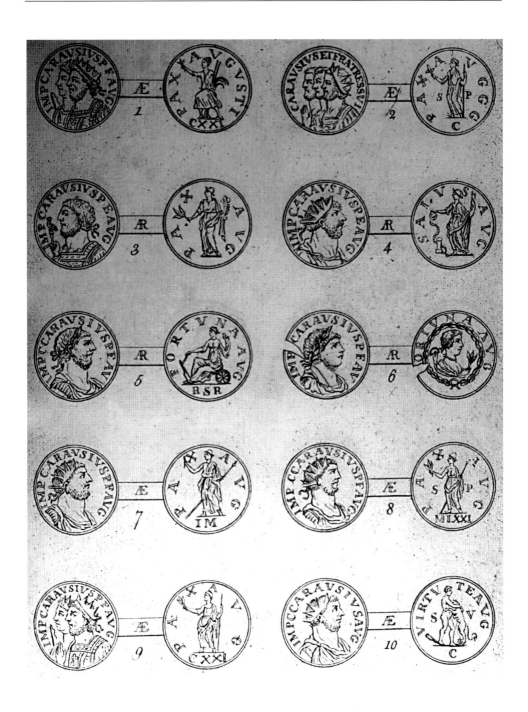

40   *Coins of Carausius.* From W. Stukeley, *The Medallic History of Marcus Aurelius*
     Valerius Carausius, Emperor of Brittain, 1757

evidence for some enlargement of villas in the countryside and a modest number of mosaics are now being ascribed to this period. It is likely that Britain benefited from being part of the Gallic Empire, under the rule of men with Gaulish antecedents, such as Postumus, Victorinus and the Tetrici, and it would be surprising if some Britons did not rise to positions of importance in their courts. But the military problems of the time lay largely along the Rhine and, if Britain was secure, it was inevitably something of a political backwater.

Some piracy existed along the east coast, probably an endemic problem though this did give the commander of the channel fleet some influence. One such commander, a Menapian (from Belgium) called Mauseus Carausius staged a coup in 286 seizing a large section of northern Gaul and evidently securing the active compliance of the British. He made London the epicentre of his rule and struck a coinage which if in part based on that of the Gallic Empire, appealed directly to the interests of the provincial élite. First by striking in pure silver he signalled a return to financial stability; second while his common coin types signalled peace and stability, other coins display Vergilian catchphrases from the *Aeneid* or from Eclogue 4, which the educated classes in Britain would certainly have learned at school. At last the 'long awaited' saviour had come; the rule of Saturn – the Golden Age – was restored. He strengthened the defences of the coastal forts, and the splendid and well-preserved walls of Portchester with their bastions may well be of his time.

Carausius is portrayed dressed in consular robes on some of his coins and medallions; there was nothing unusual in an emperor being shown so magnificently arrayed, but no emperor had ever before had the chance to show himself in London in this Late-Roman style. We must envisage a hastily convened senate in London composed in many instances of British men of substance. Even when Carausius was overthrown and killed in a coup in 293, his successor Allectus continued this tradition of strong local rule, though his coins stress the importance of ships as the threat of an offensive from the Central Empire came closer.

An interlude. London. October 287.

Primus was wearing a new toga, embellished with the broad purple stripe of a senator. He and his wife Vicina had travelled in comfort from Corinium to the capital. He was to sit in the newly reconditioned senate house, once the curia of London, and hear a panegyric delivered by one of his colleagues to the Unconquered Augustus, Marcus Aurelius Mausaeus Carausius. It would be full of Vergilian tags extolling the 'long awaited one', the 'restorer of Saturn's golden age'. These seemed apt to Primus.

Afterwards he and Vicina were to go together to a reception the Emperor had laid on for all the most influential men of the two British provinces.

Vicina had given him a jewelled gold brooch to mark the twentieth anniversary of their marriage. He had spent some time in a jeweller looking at onyx cameos, some of ladies with low-cut dresses inscribed in Greek 'To the beautiful girl!'. It did not seem right really, certainly not if Vicina was to wear it in the palace, even if it was only the former governor's palace. The jeweller had then shown him a lovely pendant made of black jet from Yorkshire showing a man and a woman looking affectionately at one another. The pair looked like them; furthermore the reverse was cut with the clasped hands of concord.

Vicina, too, viewed the evening with anticipation. Her husband had looked splendid as a senator. She knew that she was the more practical of the two. Primus was always daydreaming, writing poetry. It was she who had fixed the route to allow Primus to meet the factor of his estate south of Alchester, Alauna the holy, who had begun to make pottery on a large scale. Tamesubugus was a sound businessman and was running the estate well. Vicina's main interest was in pilgrimage. They had managed to attend the festival of Mercury at Alauna, and enjoyed an excellent joint of lamb after the sacrifice, and some reasonable wine.

Despite the crowds, as a senator on his way to greet the Emperor, he and Vicina were able to stay at the spacious *mansio* rather than try pot luck at an inn. There, the baths were always clean, reasonably commodious and the ambience was relaxing. They sat in the courtyard garden in the evening and watched the sun go down.

Then they proceeded on to Verulamium where Vicina's relatives lived. She was a Catuvellaunian. She wanted very much to attend the festival of the local Mars, but was a bit fearful of what Primus would say. Verulamium had been an allied city from the beginning. The law said human sacrifice was forbidden. However, serious crimes could be punished by death. What happened at Verulamium was that these were combined. This year a highwayman, a member of a Bagaudae gang, had been captured. He had certainly killed two people if not three and would clearly have to pay for his crimes. Here he was paraded through the theatre, taken along the processional way to the top of the hill where the great temple tomb of the last king of Verulamium was situated and beheaded. The non-Roman element was the defleshing of the skull and its exhibition in the temple. Primus's first reaction had been disgust, but he then started to think of all the sacrifices of mortal men he remembered in verse: Iphigenia, Pentheus, the prisoners Achilles had killed on the tomb of Patroclus; and even in modern Italy the rites of the priesthood of Nemi where the new priest kills the old priest. This was a diverse Empire.

Vicina's cousin Lucilla and her husband Censorinus were forthright. 'There has always been a problem with highwaymen', Censorinus said. 'The municipality or the state should do something about it! What are soldiers for? Beneficiarii aren't just there to feed horses and count official letters . . . Well maybe things will be better now.'

'Some of these brigands are soldiers who deserted their units with their weapons after maybe committing a capital crime', Lucilla added. 'Do you remember what happened to aunt Regina?' She continued for the benefit of Primus and Vicina. 'Well, Regina was only fifteen and then set out towards Londinium with her companion, Severa and a male escort. They never reached Sulloniacae. They had been set on by a gang; their male servant had been hacked down. The girls had vanished. Severa was never seen again; she probably ended up in some brothel somewhere. But Barates, a trader in military standards and vexilla, a jew from Palmyra, saw Regina in chains, fell in love with her, bought her, liberated her and married her.'

41   *The tombstone of the Catuvellaunian woman, Regina, wife of Barates the Palmyrene, from South Shields, Co. Durham*

'All in one day, according to aunt', said Lucilla. 'They were very happy. Lived mainly in the north but visited us here each year. I remember, as a girl, Aunt Regina would tell me to be very kind to slaves because no one knew her own fate or thought a Catuvellaunian could become a slave. She had been very, very lucky. But even Barates with his marvellous contacts could never trace Severa . . . Poor aunt, she died after about 15 years of marriage, at Arbeia in the north. Childbirth complications I think, despite the charm she was wearing. Barates was heart-broken. He set up a wonderful tombstone carved by one of his countrymen and had it inscribed in Latin and Aramaic. "Regina, the freedwoman of Barates, alas!" We saw Barates only once afterwards, he was a changed man . . . very sad and shrunken. He gave me some of auntie's jewellery, this fine open-work pendant and a gold ring inscribed "*Iunoni Mea*", and the haemetite charm with the image of Isis and a representation of a womb – a sentimental keepsake but clearly a dud, because it didn't save auntie. Shortly afterwards poor Barates went back to the Wall, and died at Coria, we gather.'

'I suppose', said Censorinus, 'the brigands, in a manner of speaking, introduced us to Barates and all worked out well up to a point for Regina, but that does not mean that the whole pack of brigands should not have been sacrificed, to Nemesis if to no other deity! We are humane people in Verulamium, but there are limits to our tolerance.'

Pilgrimage to Alauna and Verulamium had been the hors d'oeuvre. Politics was the climax. Vicina and Primus watched the emperor, massive and bull-necked but with a well manicured, curly beard full of gold dust, a Gallienus then, not an Aurelian. His expression was genial and his speech surprisingly cultivated and gentle. By contrast his finance minister, Allectus, who stood behind looked like a thug despite the full beard which attempted to make him look like Marcus Aurelius. The perceptive Vicina was chilled by his eyes.

She joined Primus as they walked hand in hand along the rose-petal-strewn streets to the old governor's palace, now the centre of power of this little Empire. Primus exclaimed 'We knew the old Gallic Empire of Postumus, Victorinus, and the Tetrici when we were young. Those Gauls were people just like us and they sympathised with our problems, but we never saw them!'

'No', said Vicina, 'but your brother Sempronius did go to Cologne and Trier and gave as a glowing account of Gallic magnificence, and of Gallic oratory . . . a sort of civilised version of what went on before we became Romans.'

'Do you call what we saw three days ago at Verulamium "civilised"?', said Primus. 'Still, let that pass. It worked and it will work here provided', and he laughed nervously, 'the barbarians don't walk in.'

'Barbarians?', queried Vicina.

'Yes . . . this time the barbarians are the Roman army, maybe for the first time; if they come we will have to watch out . . .'

The effects of the invasion led by Constantius Chlorus and his commander Asclepiodotus in 296 and the subsequent death of Allectus were doubtless severe, as far as the better off citizens of the British provinces were concerned. A medallion calls Constantius Chlorus the 'Restorer of the Eternal Light' but it was struck in Trier. Although the mint at London was maintained for the time being, it struck only standardised issues. Allectan coin hoards and the likelihood that a number of villas end at this time suggest the reality. A century before, when Albinus was killed, there were reprisals which fell of course on men of property. One possible victim of the purge was Alban at Verulamium. The Christian saint may be an accretion from various sources (including a pre-existing Celtic hero venerated on the nearby hill at Folly Lane as well as a historical figure who died violently). The date of his death is uncertain, but if he perished under Constantius the date would agree near enough with the famous great persecution of Diocletian, though his 'crime' was more probably subversion than adherence to Christianity.

We are better informed about the fourth century than the third. At first sight there seems to be a real dichotomy between the wealth of the villas and town houses – with their mosaics and collections of silver plate and jewellery – and the bastion-enhanced town walls, all of which befitted the 'golden age' of Roman Britain, and the frequent revolts, showing that the power of central Empire was increasingly resented by the provincials. However, there was no hint of the crude 'nationalism' of the Boudican revolt but rather British Romans, often men of culture and somewhat old fashioned *humanitas*, found themselves increasingly resenting rule by men of military stock from the Balkans.

Historians have tended to treat Constantius Chlorus and his son Constantine far too kindly. Constantine as the first Christian emperor was regarded benignly by Church historians like Bishop Eusebius; by extension even Constantius had to be a 'good' man, reluctant to persecute Christians. In fact what we know of Constantine shows him to have been a ruthless, blood-soaked tyrant who did not scruple to murder his wife and eldest son. There is no evidence that he was popular in Britain and the fact that 'Adventus' coins were struck on two occasions in London suggests that his presence was required in this restless island to prevent trouble.

Constantine's most momentous decision, apart from throwing his influence behind Christianity, was to found a new capital far to the east at Constantinople (*c*.AD 324).

42a   Regular Urbs Roma *issue of Constantine, showing head of Roma and wolf and twins*

People would have known about this division of the Empire from a vast emission of low denomination coins celebrating 'Constantinopolis' together with another vast issue with the legend '*Urbs Roma*'. These coins were widely used and unofficially widely copied in Britain, and although we cannot prove that the helmeted head of Roma on the obverse and the Roman wolf suckling Romulus and Remus on the reverse had especial resonance amongst the hagglers in the market place, who were hardly the cultural elite, it is very possible that for many the type symbolised the identity the British provincials felt with Roman culture if not with Roman politics.

We next hear of Britain in 340 when his son Constans was impelled to rush over to Britain in the middle of winter. This was not the campaigning season so the emergency is most likely to have been internal dissent, even open revolt. Then only 10 years later Britain was at the epicentre of the revolt of Magnentius, whose mother is said to have been a Briton. Evidently many of the landowners supported him, and the thoroughness of British involvement is shown in the aftermath of the revolt which ended when Magnentius was defeated in battle at Mursa on the Danube in 353. He fled to the West but further resistance proved in vain and he subsequently committed suicide at Lyons. Constantius II clearly blamed quite a number of influential Britons. He sent a secret agent called Paulus to implicate as many as possible in treason. Even the governor Martinus was forced to commit suicide, an event which the historian Ammianus Marcellinus (XIV, 5, 6-8) declared 'cast an indelible stain on the reign of Constantius'. The hatred felt by some of the provincials to the House of Constantine is shown by a number of coins of the dynasty overstruck at this time in the name of *Domino Carausius C(a)es(ar)*. Although it is just possible that there was an unknown usurper called Carausius, it is more likely that these coins merely extol the 'good old days' of the British emperor, rather as Jacobite tokens did

42b British copy of Urbs Roma *coin. Both coins from Woodeaton.*
Photos: Institute of Archaeology, Oxford, courtesy Adrian Marsden

in the eighteenth century. Several villas in Hampshire and Gloucestershire have coin lists which end at this time, including Thruxton, so Quintus Natalius Natalinus may have been one of those who fell victim to the purges and show trials.

Some of the towns of Roman Britain were provided with impressive bastions in the middle years of the fourth century, including Chichester, Cirencester and Caerwent, those at the last two towns being heptagonal in shape. Designed to reflect enhanced status as much as to aid defence, were these the result of an Imperial grant (perhaps even by Magnentius) or of the efforts of vigorous patrons, who could curry favour with even the most difficult of emperors? It could be claimed that both Cirencester and Caerwent were at their apogee in the fourth century. The splendidly conserved circuit of the latter, the finest walls in Britannia Prima, and perhaps the entire province, dating to the last years of Constantine (*c.*AD 330) with bastions added 20 years later, express the continuing confidence in city life still felt well into the fourth century.

There was an ironical end to the fifty-year history of the frightful Constantinian dynasty. Its last member, Julian, was not an illiterate boor like his predecessors, but a gentle Greek scholar who fell under the suspicion of the jealous Constantius and was packed off west to face the invincible barbarians who had breached the Rhine frontier, nominally as junior Emperor (Caesar). Quoting Homer's lines about 'purple death' this untried boy led a brilliant campaign, smashing the German armies. He reduced taxation in Gaul and also in Britain, where it is clear some taxation was forming a source of illicit personal income for certain generals in the army (Libanius, *Orations* 18, 82). Julian's friend, Alypius, was usefully positioned as Vicarius in Britain. The Caesar managed to detach his 'minder' Lupercinus, sent by Constantius to spy on him, and despatched him to Britain supposedly to deal with incursions of the Scots and Picts (Ammianus Marcellinus XX, 1). The account suggests the danger may have been quite imaginary, as it generally was. Lupercinus was sent in the middle of winter; he crossed from Boulogne to Richborough and then to London, hardly the best place from which to deal with trouble in Pictland! No doubt Alypius and the Britons did the rest, as was demanded of them. One day early in 361 a letter arrived in Britain from Julian to Alypius, an invitation, it seemed, to an aristocratic hunt in the Isle de France: 'there is much hunting of small deer here'. It was the coded signal for revolt. Julian, proclaimed Augustus by his men and raised on a shield, marched south and east against Constantius. What the result would have been if Constantius (who inevitably had the larger army) had lived we do not know but Constantius died unexpectedly of fever at Tarsus on 5 October.

Julian's sole reign was, alas for Britain and the Empire in general, very short – he died fighting the Sasanian Persians in 363 – but its effects in Britain, especially in the religious sphere, were to last for the rest of the century. The Julianic revolution – it was no less – was an appeal to a traditional society, cultured and aristocratic, based on pagan ideals. It is reflected in Britain in mosaics like those at Littlecote and the temple at Lydney and in other similar works of art. Had Julian not been killed harmony might well have been restored in a province which was so wedded to the old-fashioned virtues.

As it was there was only a brief interval under Valentinian I, Julian's proximate successor, before in 364 there was, once more, major trouble; Ammianus writes of attacks by Picts, Saxons, Scots and Attacotti harassing the Britons with continual calamities (Ammianus Marcellinus XXVI, 4.5) but the troubles were probably more complex and came to a head in 367. Ammianus' account (XXVII, 8) is certainly rather confused. An important officer Nectaridus, the *comes* in charge of the maritime district, had been killed and the *dux*, Fullofaudes, had been ambushed and taken prisoner. In the aftermath of this disaster another *comes*, Theodosius, father of the emperor, was sent, landed at Richborough and went on to London (which Ammian tells us was later called Augusta). Here he is said to have dealt with marauding bands of enemy laden with booty and asked for new governors to be sent out. However Ammianus also tells us about a political exile in Britain called Valentinus who stirred up a revolt against Count Theodosius (XXVIII, 3). This was suppressed and Valentinus was executed although Count Theodosius 'forbade enquiries being made into the conspiracy so as to prevent fear from spreading widely and reawakening in the province those tensions that had been lulled to sleep'.

It seems not unlikely that the entire account deals with events that have very little if anything to do with outside barbarians and everything to do with a hostile and reasonably well organised Romano-British ruling class, perhaps paying mercenaries. The epicentre of the revolt may actually have been in Britannia Prima, the Cirencester region of Gloucestershire and in North Wiltshire. The well-defended centre of Cunetio (Mildenhall) with its close-set bastions has been seen as a Valentinianic fortress. There is quite a high concentration of Valentinianic coins in the region and in neighbouring Gloucestershire. A silver finger-ring from

Roundway Down with an imperial portrait and the legend *NIKE* (Victory) in Greek may have belonged to a leading member of the Count's army. Very probably London was renamed Augusta at this time, the loyal capital of Maxima and Count Theodosius' headquarters. By 369 Britain (including *Prima*) was apparently quiet, but clearly the populace were not reconciled to the arbitrary rule of soldiers who shared nothing of their culture.

In 382 Magnus Maximus, of Spanish origin and the leading army commander in Britain, was made emperor by his troops and took an army to Gaul where he overthrew and killed Valentinian's son Gratian (Orosius, *Adversum Paganos* VII, 34.9-10; Zosimus IV, 35, 2-6). To what extent he had a following amongst civilians is uncertain. On the one hand his fanatical Christianity would not have appealed; on the other he did leave an impression in British (Welsh) folklore as the good emperor Mascen Wledig. He lingered in London long enough to open a mint striking gold coins with the '*Augusta*' mintmark and he probably initiated the construction of a cathedral in the eastern part of the city. The rest of Maximus' reign was occupied in civil war on the Continent culminating in his defeat and death at the hands of the new emperor Theodosius at Aquileia in 388.

The last decade of the fourth century presents us with few firm facts; simply around 400 a supposed 'victory' by Stilicho. The poet Claudian (*De. cons. Stilichonis* II, 247-55) has Britannia 'dressed in the skin of a Caledonian beast, her cheeks tattooed and her blue mantle swathed over her feet like the Ocean's surge'. She goes on to thank Stilicho for protecting her from the Picts and Scots, though in truth there is no reason at all to believe that Stilicho conducted any such campaign in the north or ever came to the Province. Thus we find the revival of familiar symbols by an Empire increasingly centred on the problems of southern and eastern Europe. This was the scenario for the final rupture with the Roman state.

A letter from Quintus Natalius Natalinus to his daughter Severa, Thruxton. Autumn A.D 354.

My beloved child, I staked all on Magnentius, a decent man who was not avaricious for money, was tolerant to all despite those big chi-rho coins, and cared for Britain. After his death some said that the great Emperor Carausius had a son, hidden by the gods in a sacred grove and now riding out to victory over the forces of darkness. I was one of those who proclaimed Our Lord Carausius in Venta. As a result the agent of that snake Constantius, Paulus 'the chain' is after me and I know my life must shortly end in one way or another. As a believer in the true and undiminished radiance of the gods, I will take my own life before the scoundrels drag me off and torture me. I send my love and a brooch. I have broken my ring which it would be too dangerous to bequeath.

I know we will meet again in Elysium; may the usurper Constantius and his foul agents rot in Tartarus. Farewell and may the gods protect you through life.

A proclamation of the Lord *praeses*, Lucius Septimius. Enacted at Corinium. September AD 360.

Our great and glorious Emperor, Julianus, revokes and repeals all impediments to religious observance made against the will of the gods. In accord with his desire and on my own account too, the columns of Jupiter will once again grace our Forum. On the day of inauguration a solemn sacrifice will be made to the god in expiation of our recent impiety. The columns will be set up once again in Glevum; in Venta Belgarum; in Noviomagus Regnensium and in all other cities of our province.

Temple record. Lydney AD 387 November.

The priest Titus Flavius Senilis makes a deposition to the effect that it is becoming increasingly hard to maintain sacrifices in the face of hostility from the State (even though the *praeses* of Prima turns a blind eye to our rites) and there is a severe shortage of cash. The cost of maintaining the building rises each year and it is incredible that less than 20 years ago we had sufficient funds from worshippers to lay a new mosaic.

If we cannot continue the gods will surely desert us or bring war and pestilence on mortal men for impiety . . . and even now I see these everywhere. Maxen assailed us but I gather he is even now engaged in mortal combat with Theodosius. Whatever happens cannot be good. Maxen is a bigot; Theodosius is the offspring of the cruel *comes* of that name who harried Britain and slew so many of our best men of Britannia Prima on the specious pretext that 'we were siding with the barbarian Saxons and Picts and had created a conspiracy' . . .

(this is the last official entry on the scroll but inserted in another hand below it . . .)

Victorinus ex visu. I have dreamed and seen. Nodens came to me with the entire assembly of the gods. He spoke: 'Good and faithful servant, the tribulations of Britain will soon end. The gods fulfil themselves in many ways and under many names!'

And the Lord Apollo spoke: 'I am ruler of the seasons, and the dancing years. I have many names. I am the hound-prince, the great deliverer, the protector, the Unconquered Sun whom the Persians call Mithras, the divine archer, the Lord of music and the dance. I have united with my brother Bacchus to bring peace to the island.'

Then Bacchus proclaimed his many names and powers: 'As Faunus, the mighty, the protector, the guardian of treasure; as Pan, king of the wild places and in my own name Lord of the Vine and the fountain of Life. With Apollo I bring inspiration and music to men. You have often seen me in the image of my servant Orpheus who combines the attributes of Apollo with my own person and keeps us from conflict. Though you, as a mortal, cannot see far into the future, the divine powers admonish you not to despair! The spring is not yet dry; the glorious dwellings of the gods will once again arise!'

And then I awoke . . .

6 The cycle of the turning year

15 September AD 361.

Lucius Septimius, rector or governor of Britannia Prima, had just bathed after sacrificing to the gods. He was giving a dinner party at his great villa at Woodchester, some miles from Corinium. Staying with him were three men, with glowing reputations throughout the province. Bellicus had been adopted by a childless landowner called Saturninus and left a large and very attractive estate at Stonesfield. Young Claudianus came from Littlecote and was already expanding his property, building a new cult room beside a little stream. Candidus was now regarded as the leading mosaicist of Corinium and was also Bellicus' best and oldest friend.

Standing in the inner garden and enjoying the soft western sun which illuminated the soft pink petals of some late Autumn Damask roses, Vergil's Paestan roses, and sipping chilled honeyed wine, *mulsum*, from silver cups, each chased with a different scene from myth, concerning the loves and metamorphoses of the gods, they began talking.

Lucius, as the host, started by praising the enormous floor of his reception room, which showed Orpheus surrounded by friezes of birds and of animals, all enthralled by the music of his lyre. In the outer spandrels were the nymphs who seemed to be swimming in the splashing water of the fountain. 'It was not my commission, you understand; rather it was the choice of one of my predecessors. I have never seen anything quite like it before. I gather that you rather go in for such circular designs here in this province?'

'Certainly we do', said Bellicus. 'My own villa has a mosaic which shows Bacchus presiding over nature, indicated by birds which stand for the sky and the cooling breezes and also by a head of Neptune symbolising the life-giving waters. I know that, because my friend Candidus here actually worked on it with his father, over twenty years ago. Actually they designed and made your floors too!'

Candidus blushed, almost to the colour of the roses. 'It was really all the work of my dear old father, Severus', he said. 'But it is an interesting story all the same. Normally, as you know, a mosaicist simply reproduces ideas given to him by the patron who employs him, the old opposition between *techne* and *paedeia*. But Severus was learned, self-taught but with a questing mind. He made sure I went to school and it was at school that I met Bellicus. Everyone was full of the revived Platonic philosophy of Plotinus and talking of 'the still centre, the ground of our being, around which all life and even the heavenly bodies move'. Our local hunter-god was often compared to Orpheus by the students and one day father heard Bellicus and myself arguing that they were one and the same god. He said nothing but sat there, just sketching on a tablet, deep in thought. Then came the great commission and somehow he persuaded the authorities that his was the best design for an Orpheus mosaic. As the governor's palace, I suppose there is no real owner in the usual sense, just the current *praeses* and his advisors.'

'My mosaic room, which Candidus here had laid for me, in a different, more modern style, after having taken on some mosaic-workers from Durnovaria, also shows Orpheus', said Claudianus. 'It serves me as a shrine. In the centre is Orpheus as you have here, but after a long talk we both agreed that the composition should equate him both with Bacchus and with Apollo, for Orpheus is the prophet of them both.'

Candidus butted in, for Claudianus was far too good a friend to treat with the usual deference due to a patron. 'I have reconciled the mind and the body, the spirit and the flesh. I show the changing seasons, the transformation of Bacchus when he fled from the Titans, when he died and when he was resurrected as we will surely be reborn after death . . .'

'We will indeed', replied Bellicus, reciting slowly in Greek. '"I am the child of earth and of the starry heavens. Give me to drink lest I perish."'

'I see,' said Lucius. 'Even in Gaul, in Reims my birthplace, we unhesitatingly speak of Britain without thinking about the island as it is. We picture it as "a half barbarous land beyond Ocean", and we personify it as a savage woman with long, unkempt hair, wearing a torque and trousers. We inhabit it at best with half-literate soldiers, at worst with boorish Britons; but you all seem to be more Roman than we are, or perhaps more Greek for I have learned more about Platonic philosophy here than I have in Italy . . . but I should have realised, Candidus, for the device on the gem you wear in your signet-ring is a bust of Socrates.'

Candidus laughed. 'Socrates warns us not to look at the exterior which in his case was uncouth, like a Silenus, but at the inner man. If you look back at our histories I think you will find that far less separates us from you than you think; certainly far less than separates us from those coarse soldiers whoever they are, and wherever they come from.'

Art in late Roman Britain was concerned with religious beliefs, with the language and myth of the dominant culture and with the ceremony which surrounded the lives of the élite. If there was nothing new in this integration of education and its visual representation, it was given its most graphic expression in the fourth century, notably in mosaics but also in wall-painting and on silverware.

The workshops, which sent out teams of men to lay mosaics and paint the walls of the villas, were based in towns, including Corinium, Chichester, Winchester, Dorchester in Dorset and Ilchester in Britannia Prima as well as in other provinces, at Leicester and Water Newton, plausibly in Britannia Secunda and at Aldborough, possibly in Flavia Caesariensis. One of the first sumptuous villa complexes of the fourth century is not so many miles from Fishbourne, whose life had come to an end as a rich man's residence in the troubles of the third century, perhaps at the time of the invasion of Constantius in 296. The mosaic-floored suites at Bignor in the Sussex

Downs are only about 20 years later and in their sumptuous gentility and erudition they set the tone for the 'Golden Age' of Romano-British art. They were probably laid by a workshop based in Chichester or Winchester which developed a highly distinctive style. We know nothing for certain about the organisation of the team except that one of the minor floors in a corridor bears a representation of a dolphin and the abbreviated name Terentius (*RIB* 2448.11), presumably not the master designer of the whole but an apprentice.

The grandest chamber, perhaps a winter dining-room because it had an efficient system of underfloor heating, is dominated by an apse containing a head and shoulder 'portrait' of Venus in a roundel. Her long elegant hair leaves no doubt of her identification. The nimbus around her head emphasises her divine power, the power of love. There is a hint that this is more than just a representation of the goddess. This Venus surely also represents the *domina*, the lady of the house who would have presided here. The Venus roundel is hung with garlands on which perch long-tailed pheasants, sacred to her. (Incidentally we probably owe the introduction of these birds into Britain to the Romans.) A scroll of vegetation grows from a wine cup and surrounds the entire panel. Below we see a frieze of cupids dressed as glad-iators, a conceit which in this case merely alludes to the pains of love – and of life itself. The main part of the floor no doubt had a central roundel too but that is lost; all you have around are panels of cupids or corybants, dancing with shields. Probably Mars occupied the centre as he is shown in precisely the same position in the midst of martial cupids on a floor at Fullerton, Hampshire. He would represent the master of the house, the *dominus*. The theme of the lovemaking of Mars and Venus was a popular myth, described in book four of Ovid's *Metamorphoses*, for example. It may be the theme of the elaborate wall-painting decorating a small villa-like building at what seems to be the centre of a small Imperial estate at Kingscote, Gloucestershire.

The summer dining-room at Bignor has a hexagonal fountain at its centre, surrounded by six figures of maenads. Here, too, is a wonderful representation of Ganymede being snatched up to Heaven by Jupiter, disguised as an eagle. Ovid describes the scene in book ten of the *Metamorphoses*. The god was on fire for the love of a Phrygian shepherd-boy and turned himself into an eagle: beating the air with his borrowed wings he snatched up the shepherd of Troy, who even now mixes the wine and supplies him with nectar to the annoyance of Juno. The divine cup-bearer is a suitable subject for a dining room. Later in the century it would have embarrassed prudish Christians who not only disliked pagan stories but were scandalised by the homosexual implications of the story. The owner of the great villa at Bignor was clearly not a Christian, and probably not in the least concerned about personal sexual morality. After all desire was a gift of the gods. However, he may well have interpreted the scene as representing the flight of the soul after death to the heavens. Certainly the myth is one that is found on grave monuments with this meaning.

There was always a strong element of mystery cult in the observances of the élite. The mosaics of an extensive villa at Brading on the Isle of Wight, not far away but not the work of the Bignor mosaicists, provide an insight into the esoteric thought of the patrons of these great works of art, even if there is no agreement amongst those who

43   Lycurgus strangled by Ambrosia (the Vine).
Detail of mosaic at Brading, Isle of Wight.
Photo: Institute of Archaeology, Oxford

have studied them on what they meant. The largest chamber is divided into an antechamber, very defective but showing in the one remaining panel Perseus and Andromeda. Perseus uses the head of Medusa to turn evil forces to stone and the apotropaic (life-giving) Medusa head occupies the central roundel in the larger portion of the room. How does one access this life? Around it are four rectangular panels each containing two figures. One shows a man with a double axe assailing a female figure. He is Lycurgus, enemy of Bacchus; she is Bacchus' votary, the maenad Ambrosia. Bacchus will transform her into a vine which will strangle her persecutor. Then there is Attis and the nymph Sangaritis, Demeter giving the seed corn to Triptolemos and probably Apollo and Daphne. These symbolise the great mystery cults of Dionysos-Bacchus, Attis and Cybele, Demeter and Apollo. The astronomer, astrologer or holy man with his globe and sundial between them mediates between earth and heaven in the trance techniques known as theurgy, practised amongst others by the great Plotinus. Another floor depicts in the central roundel a bust of Bacchus. In one side panel is a man with the head of a cockerel, a house reached by a ladder and two griffins. This has been seen by some as a blundered hunting scene, but it is far more likely that it to has a specific religious meaning. The figure helps man to reach safety in a world beset by spiritual hazards. He might well be Iao who Praetextatus in Macrobius' *Saturnalia* describes as the 'greatest of all gods', though on amulets Iao usually has serpentiform feet; he could be Hermes Trismegistos, 'thrice-great Hermes'. He was balanced by another figured panel, though the main subject is now lost; however key to his identity is provided by a fox who bounds towards a circular building. Was the missing figure Orpheus? A similar fox is shown on a threshold panel in the villa which depicts Orpheus and the animals. The general meaning of this part of the floor is given by a gladiatorial scene, emphasising the struggles of life. Incidentally, this and a panel of cupid gladiators at Brading are the only appearances of this subject in fourth-century British mosaic. In contrast to other provinces, the near total lack of interest in the arena is profound. Here gladiators simply provide convenient metaphors.

The interlocking of religion, classical culture and ceremonial can be illustrated most clearly with regard to a group of mosaics, mentioned briefly in the previous chapter, linked by subject and design. These are circular mosaics showing Orpheus

44   The mosaic at Littlecote, Wiltshire showing the turning seasons

and the beasts found predominantly in south-west Britain but with a few outliers in Yorkshire and north Lincolnshire. The myth of Orpheus, whose singing charmed the animals and even the furies of the underworld, had a wide appeal. Orpheus is a saviour, who amongst the Jews (on a mosaic at Gaza for instance) could be equated with King David and amongst the Christians with Christ, and he is not uncommon on Roman mosaics throughout the Empire. However, the type of circular floor in which Orpheus is placed at the hub of a circle while animals and birds perambulate outside would appear to have been invented in Britain, probably in Cirencester around AD 300 or a decade or so afterwards. Its popularity was no doubt in part owing to the prevalence of philosophical beliefs of Platonic origin amongst the provincial élite. As the world turns and the seasons change there is a still, unchanging centre. At Newton St Loe near Bath, upon a mosaic now in Bristol Museum, the animals are still unsubdued as though Orpheus has just arrived on the scene, but at Barton Farm outside Cirencester and at the palatial villa at Woodchester, Gloucestershire the concentric registers of animals and birds slink around as though hypnotised by his lyre. The Woodchester floor was a very grand reception room in which Orpheus was offset from the centre probably by a fountain, and this watery theme is taken up by representations of nymphs in the spandrels at the corners, linking Orpheus with the water of life, and perhaps with the Orphic idea that after death Orpheus' adherents would drink from the 'well of memory' to achieve immortality. However unlikely it might seem for such a very public room to have major religious significance, it is to view with our own eyes and, as we shall see, Orpheus floors certainly had a profoundly spiritual meaning elsewhere.

   This sophisticated composition, like all the British Orpheus pavements, includes a native element in its iconography. Orpheus with his hound or fox closely resembles a hunter god found on sculptures in south-western Britain and in London. This deity wears a peaked cap like the oriental god Attis with whom he may sometimes have been equated, he carries a bow associated with the archer god Apollo and his sister Diana, and is often with a hound and a stag. An altar from Nettleton Shrub, Wiltshire is actually dedicated to Apollo Cunomaglus, 'the hound-prince'. Romano-British Orpheus mosaics may thus incorporate within their designs native religious ideas.

It has already been pointed out, by Sarah Scott, that it is easy to endow the arrangement of the Woodchester mosaic with a political gloss. The villa-owner (the *dominus*) stands as the earthly Orpheus while all around him his clients, servants and slaves are figured as animals circling around him and as it were paying him tribute or more probably he identified himself with the hunter-god whose taste for the chase he surely shared. Woodchester can thus very easily be regarded as having been the ceremonial epicentre of an estate, where we can imagine the *dominus* and *domina*, dressed in splendid clothes, holding court on this very spot. But such an interpretation does not negate another.

The mosaic in a small rectangular building, set on the banks of a stream at the Littlecote villa in eastern Wiltshire, treats the theme rather differently and may have served a rather different purpose. The small rectangular building with three apses would have looked rather like a church, and may have served as a sort of pagan house-chapel. Fittingly, coin evidence suggests it was built early in the 360s in the reign of the pagan emperor Julian. The mosaic's iconography is taut and elusive. Some elements are certainly Bacchic, including on one section panthers facing a cantharus and sea-panthers. Between this and the other more architecturally complex element of the floor is a panel representing water. Here in a building which was not a major public thoroughfare, an esoteric interpretation of this as the Orphic 'well of memory' is persuasive. Indeed one passes from it to the central figure of Orpheus who is accompanied, as on other British Orpheus mosaics, by a canine animal (probably a dog rather than a fox). There are only four animals portrayed cavorting around him and they are each accompanied by a human figure: Venus, Nemesis or Leda, Ceres and Persephone. They can be claimed to represent the four seasons, respectively spring, summer, autumn and winter, under the control of Apollo. They represent the changes in the turning year and the cycles of human life just as their animals, goat, fawn, leopard and bull, represent the transformations of Bacchus when he was fleeing from the Titans. The panther masks on the chords of the apses provide the points from which sun-rays burst out (or can they simply be interpreted as the ribs of pecten shells?). The thought behind this floor is probably Orphic, concerned with the reconciliation of Apollo and Bacchus in the person of Orpheus and the mystery of life, death and rebirth.

The problem we have in understanding the imagery is that these mosaics were intended for members of a tight group who shared an education, social structure and belief system that was different from our own. That is our misfortune; it was not theirs. There is no reason why the ancient viewer should have adopted an entirely idiosyncratic approach to understanding the Orpheus theme. The response would have been shared by like-minded people from the same background. Of course, eating and ceremony certainly played a part in the rites enacted at Littlecote, as they did at Woodchester, but that does not minimise the importance of religious belief to the patrons who had such mosaics laid. A mosaic called the 'Mysteries Mosaic' at Trier depicts the myth of Leda and the swan, and cult acts, dancing and feasting connected with an otherwise unknown cult based around this story. There is a possibility that the ingestion of drugs in wine, as suggested by an infuser carefully kept in a *cista mystica* from the late Roman (Bacchic) phase of the onetime Mithraeum at London (in Maxima Caesariensis), and sexual acts were part of such rituals.

Further understanding of such floors and the patronage that produced them is provided by other mosaics depicting Bacchus, perhaps the most popular pagan deity amongst the élite of late Roman Britain. A mosaic from the villa at Thruxton, Hampshire, now a somewhat sad fragment in the British Museum, had as its central device (now lost) a youthful Bacchus amidst vines, seated on a leopard which he is feeding with life-giving wine. The field around him, which remains, is circular and divided into eight divisions each containing a head wearing a Phrygian type cap. The number eight might relate to the number of days in the original Roman week, the so-called *nundinum*. In the spandrels are four busts representing the four seasons. The turning of the year, and of human life, is implicit here too. The mosaic was laid in a dining room added to a barn-like villa of native type; such an apparently simple building-type might well have lavish architectural embellishment as is shown by the surviving gable wall at Meonstoke in the same county. An inscription on the Thruxton floor names the owner of the villa; he was called Quintus Natalius Natalinus who, to judge from his name, was old-fashioned and traditional in his outlook. By the fourth century the formal *tria nomina* (nomen with a praenomen before and a cognomen after it) had been largely abandoned through most of the Empire but was still in vogue in pagan circles within Britain. (Note that the Lydney mosaic was laid for a priest called Titus Flavius Senilis, who was surely also of this villa-owning class.) The name Natalius was not a real Roman name but an artificially constructed one, showing that the villa owner was a native, presumably of the Belgae. He seems to have had clients and he associated the Bodeni (perhaps brothers) in the top line of the dedicatory inscription. Unfortunately the bottom line of inscription was very fragmentary when found, but it has been reconstructed as reading in part '*ex voto*'. While at one level the room could be interpreted as being a 'shrine' to Bacchus, at another one has to recall that Bacchus was best honoured by eating and drinking. The same meaning can be ascribed to the mosaic in a dining room at Chedworth. In three of the four spandrels, however, the seasons survive, as full-length figures. Winter is a countryman wearing the *birrus britannicus*; spring is a putto with a swallow and a basket of flowers; summer holds a basket and a garland. Eight panels containing satyrs and nymphs disporting themselves in riotous and erotic dancing are fitted into an octagonal frame; in the centre there must once have been a figure of Bacchus himself but this has long gone, a victim no doubt of the weather. A nice touch is that one of the maenads, surprised by a satyr, has dropped her syrinx (pan pipes). Such instruments do not only belong to myth. From the little villa at Shakenoak, Oxfordshire, a syrinx in clay bear the names of a pair of mortal lovers, both local to judge from their

45 *Detail of mosaic of dining-room at Chedworth, Gloucestershire showing a satyr and maenad in an erotic dance. The maenad has dropped her syrinx (pan-pipes).*
Photo: Grahame Soffe

names, Catavacus and Bellicia (*RIB* 2457.1). Not far from Shakenoak was the much more sumptuous villa of Stonesfield, famous for its mosaic, a product of the same mosaicists who laid those at Woodchester, Barton Farm and Chedworth. Here Bacchus stands with his feline (as he may have done at Chedworth) encircled by a wreath of Acanthus which includes a head of Neptune or Oceanus, as indeed does the similar wreath on the great Woodchester mosaic.

A Midsummer interlude. 20 June AD 345.

No wind stirred the leaves on the branches. The sky was pale blue and cloudless and the sun almost burned the ground out of the shade. Not a dog barked on that blazing afternoon. Most animals and most men slept. Apollo was king of the realm above; the world below was dedicated to the gods of silence. Below, just a few hundred yards from the Stonesfield villa, was a little stand of ancient oaks, which the locals believed had long ago been a druid grove, where unspeakable rites had once taken place. Now this nemet or, as the Romans would say, *nemus* was the haunt of far more kindly gods, of Pan and other country deities and of a little shrine of the Lar and of Bonus Eventus and Fortuna set up by Saturninus, lord of the estate. Four friends had taken shelter from the heat amongst the shady trees. Here was Catavacus, son of Sabinus, who tenanted the Shakenoak farm and Bellicia, the daughter of Lucillus, the bailiff of the Stonesfield estate. The two shared a terracotta pan-pipes upon which Bellicia had

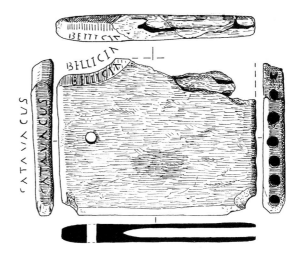

46 *The syrinx shared by Bellicia and Catavacus, found at Shakenoak, Oxfordshire. Drawing A.R. Hands*

had her name and that of her boyfriend inscribed in bold capitals. They took it in turns to play a simple, thin, reedy tune on the instrument, punctuating the concert with frequent kisses and swigs of mead fermented in the shed next to the dairy. Bellicia, who wore a chaplet of woodland flowers in honour of Venus, was currently playing, and was admittedly the better musician of the two. Their companions were Bellicus, Bellicia's brother, younger than her by little more than a year, and Candidus, son and right-hand-man of Severus, the famous mosaicist from Corinium, famous that is throughout Britannia Prima, even now laying a floor of surpassing beauty in the main room of the great villa, 'in honour of Lord Bacchus'. Nobody was working there now; Severus was enjoying a long, well-deserved siesta.

Bellicus draped a bronzed and muscular arm affectionately around Candidus' shoulder and stroked his companion's long cascading locks, 'so like those of Lord Bacchus himself', he thought, 'especially now as he had deliberately wreathed his friend's brows in ivy. What was it like to love a god?' He looked at Candidus and fancied he could see the stream of pure rays flowing from his friend's eyes into his own and linking the two of them for ever. Bellicus and Candidus were, of course, acknowledged lovers, that is their passion was acknowledged and approved by their friends and by their families. They had met over ten years ago as children at school in Corinium and saw each other frequently still, for Lucillus and his son were always there for business, and the mosaicist and the bailiff with their sons would generally meet for lunch swapping town news for country news. In fact it was Bellicus who had managed to persuade Saturninus, more of an uncle to him than a master, that Severus was just the man for a long commission at the great house. It meant a glorious summer together.

In general, life was relaxed for these young people, even in this century of conflict. Politics hardly impinged on their world and their problems were, for the most part, trivial and domestic. Bellicus had seldom been ragged at school himself, and when someone had dared to scratch on a wall, 'Candidus is a *cinaedus*, a catamite', he was soundly thrashed by Bellicus for the insult. The offender had been another boy in the school called Paulus, unpopular both because he was priggish in his morality and disrespectful to the gods. As a Christian he was an outsider in the still largely pagan town, but Christianity, once an obscure sect, had unexpectedly become the religion of the Emperor; the gods only knew why they had allowed their dignities to be insulted by non-believers! What right, anyway, had that misanthrope Paulus to blaspheme the gods who brought joy and ultimately immortality to man? Bacchus told you to dance, make love, and drink his gifts which brought on desire and made you dance!

But at least they were well away from the likes of Paulus here at the villa. Indeed, Saturninus regarded his new dining room as a sort of shrine to Bacchus. Tomorrow Candidus was privileged to lay the last few tesserae of the figured part of the floor showing the god standing beside his panther and feeding him with wine or mead; and in the evening they would dance, dressed as satyrs and maenads, arms entwined and playing pan-pipes, tibiae and cymbals just like those shown on the floor of the villa at the centre of the temple-estate at Chedworth, another masterpiece by Severus and Candidus.

The mead-cup was a simple clay vessel, a souvenir from a pilgrimage in eastern Britain. Its sides were embellished in relief by the barbotine technique with an erotic scene depicting a man with erect phallus over-excitedly approaching a bending woman and 'dropping his seed on the ground' before he reached her. It circulated as a loving-cup between the four friends . . . faster and faster as they drank to Faunus, the protector, the preserver, the mead-begotten, as well as to Bacchus and to Venus. Often at similar gatherings what was drunk was laced with herbs, sometimes blended with the drink using a silver infuser kept in a special casket. Here the four votaries were already expectant, already awaiting inspiration, and there was no need for such a concoction. They were quite steady as they rose to their feet and began to dance, at first in a haphazard, disorganised way as two separate couples; then they linked hands and began to dance in a circle, laughing and singing a catchy new song. The rondo they danced was slow and even stately at first but gradually increased in speed; their feet moved faster and faster as the tempo of their singing became louder and more confident. They were dancing to the very music of time itself, lost in the melodies of the great new hymn to love, the *Pervigilium Veneris*, which the young were singing throughout the Latin-speaking Empire. Here were fresh rhythms, never even imagined by poets before, and a revolutionary word-music, ushering in a new world of desires, both spiritual and carnal. Their scanty tunics became wet with the perspiration which ran down their faces and trickled in little rills down their backs and over their torsos. The cloth clung tightly to their bodies, and began to impede their movements. Not one of the dancers worried if some garment fell or was cast away to reveal the nudity of virile or nubile bodies which lay beneath their light, summery clothing, in the mounting tempo of the music and the urgency of the dance. As at the supreme moment of the mysteries of Bacchus when the officiant takes off the veil which hides the phallus in the *liknon*, the winnowing basket, so now chastity was discarded. Their bodies seemed intended for revelation. They were all possessed by the goddess of love! Nothing mattered save the beat of the song itself with its haunting, often repeated, refrain.

Cras amet qui nunquam amavit quique amavit cras amet:
Ver novum, ver iam canorum, ver renatus orbis est;
Vere concordant amores, vere nubunt alites,
Et nemus comam resolvit de maritis imbribus.
Cras amet qui nunquam amavit quique amavit cras amet . . .

'Tomorrow let him love who has never loved before, and let him who has loved love tomorrow. The spring is new, the spring rings with song, the spring of the world has come again. In spring lovers come together, in spring the birds couple; and the grove shakes her hair free under the marriage showers. Tomorrow let him love who has never loved before, and let him who has loved love tomorrow . . .'

The dance was at the same time intensely physical and deeply spiritual. Its motion echoed those of the stars and planets, inexorably moving on mysterious paths through the heavens. It was at once a prayer to the gods and an expression of the uncontrolled yearning the four friends had for each other, possessed as they were by a divine frenzy.

Cras amet qui nunquam amavit quique amavit cras amet.
Floreas inter coronas, myrteas inter casas,
Nec Ceres nec Bacchus absunt nec poetarum deus.
De tenente tota nox est perviglanda canticis:
Regnet in silvis Dione, tu recede Delia.
Cras amet qui nunquam amavit quique amavit cras amet.

'Tomorrow let him love who has never loved before, and let him who has loved love tomorrow. Amidst the wreaths of flowers, amongst the sprays of myrtle, Ceres and Bacchus are not absent nor is the god of poets [Apollo]. The entire night must be kept as a vigil with continuous song. Dione [mother of Venus] will reign in the woods; Depart, Delian maid [Diana, goddess of chastity]. Tomorrow let him love who has never loved before, and let him who has loved love tomorrow . . .'

The dance of the four friends recreated that of Candidus' mosaic lovers, satyrs and maenads swinging in wide circles around Lord Bacchus, playing silent instruments and singing unheard hymns to desire.

Quando fiam uti chelidon ut tacere desinam?

'When shall I be like the swallow, so that I may cease to be silent?'

Candidus thought of the little swallow perched on the right hand of spring at Chedworth. But the same ecstasy was also present in the curving sprays of acanthus with leaves of contrasting colours which Candidus had also created there and elsewhere and which encircled Orpheus at the governor's villa and the Lord Bacchus, here at Stonesfield. This rampant foliage, like the myrtle and floral wreaths of which they sang, were symbols of fecundity. All these circles he had made were designed for the swirling dance, which he was here dancing with Bellicus; and Bellicia with Catavacus and all four of them together.

Cras amet qui nunquam amavit quique amavit cras amet.

Faster and faster they danced; Lady Venus raised and raised their desires, as the song went, 'with her penetrating spirit', and Lord Bacchus too found them apt votaries of his rites, for he was assuredly here as well. The circle contracted; the dancers pressed inwards on each other and once again split apart, into their original couples. Lip met lip and tongue snaked round tongue in passionate kisses, while below thigh clasped thigh and their sacred parts touched and trembled. They knew each other; they were at one with each other. All they awaited was the moment of knowledge, of revelation, of ecstasy and of orgasm. They came . . . and the god came! This was the sanctified climax of their hymn of praise to Venus and the other ever-ruling gods.

Ipsa venas atque mentem permeanti spiritu
Intus occultis gubernat procreatrix viribus.
Ipsa Troianos nepotes in Latinos transtulit,
Romuleas ipsa fecit cum Sabinis nuptias.

'The procreator with her hidden powers controls body and mind inwardly with her penetrating soul. She transfused her Trojan progeny into the Latin people and she herself brought about the marriage of Romulus' sons with the Sabine women.'

So the song in praise of Venus at last ended, with the inevitable triumph of the goddess. Like captives in a Roman triumphal sculpture, they fell, utterly exhausted; but at the same time they felt at peace and purified rather than conquered or violated. There, upon the grass under the spreading oaks, they slept, still entwined in each others' arms, in perfect tranquility until evening when a slight chill in the air woke them.

Bellicia was the first to break silence with a ritual acclamation, taken from the rites of the Great Mother but which seemed appropriate here: 'I have eaten from the tambourine; I have drunk from the cymbal.'

Her lover responded, not directly to her but to Bellicus. 'You remember how, when we were still boys at Corinium, old Diogenes told us about Plotinus who revived Platonic philosophy about a century ago. Plotinus said "those who take part in any sacred rite must first purify themselves, discard their clothes and go up naked to the god!".'

'Oh well', interjected Bellicus with a smile, 'we have done that at least. Plotinus described God as "the still, indivisible centre of our being". It is as though he was standing in the middle of a circle and all of life whirls about him but he does not change though he can infuse us all with ecstasy, with longing, with desire . . .'

'That is exactly it', agreed Candidus. 'Only of course Plato said it first, for instance in the *Phaedrus* and the *Symposium*, long before Plotinus. We have seen and felt just for an instant, through our individual sexual desires, the absolute beauty which exists and has existed for ever, uncontaminated and unchanged. We are inevitably part of that beauty, united with it for ever, beyond this life and beyond the time when this little province of the Empire shall have changed for ever. We have been singing Venus' song but sometimes thinking of Bacchus who we celebrate tomorrow. Father and I have been trying to say in mosaic what the philosophers said in words. Sometimes with Venus, but more often with Orpheus or Lord Bacchus, we put the image of the god in the very centre of a circle. Sometimes satyrs and maenads dance around Bacchus, and there are always animals around Orpheus. This is the divine dance in which we have been taking part and continue to take part! Sometimes we include the seasons too, to show how the dance continues from season to season. No doubt some people just put their muddy feet on our floors without thinking they mean anything, which is sad, but that sort of ignorance does not make them less true. I wonder whether after even the splendid Stonesfield villa has fallen down, our mosaic to Bacchus might not survive and intrigue and instruct some future generation in say a thousand or two thousand years in the future. At least the fate of Pentheus will never touch Britain.'

They rose to their feet, laughing at the thought, and gathered up their fallen clothes from the various parts of the grove and dressed in a more or less seemly fashion. Bellicia picked up the pipes and started playing a soothing pastoral tune; the others plucked some green shoots to decorate the Bacchus room for tomorrow's ceremony. Then they slowly returned to the villa. Nothing would ever be the same again. They had come as close as mortals can come to touching god; they felt purified and saw each other as transfigured beings, held together in the unity of one spirit. The great, thousand-year-old trees had seen so much in their time, but perhaps in all those ages, never so much of sexual enjoyment; never so much of love or of true reverence for the gods. And tomorrow, for the four friends, inseparable companions and members by initiation of a life-long conventus, the dancing would begin all over again, upon the mosaic floor dedicated to Lord Bacchus. Tomorrow Candidus would complete his masterwork; tomorrow, indeed, was to be another great day, an unforgettable day, the greatest day of the fourth century, here at Stonesfield!

The realms of Bacchus (and evidently his servant Orpheus) and of Neptune were often considered in tandem. This juxtaposition is evidently the theme of the mosaics at Frampton, Dorset, where two rooms have Bacchic pavements. One figures him within a roundel, seated on a panther and flanked on each side with a panel showing a hunting scene. The other shows the god standing, holding a bunch of grapes perhaps for his panther. Around him in each corner is a wind god, and between these four scenes mentioned in the last chapter and three, at least, evidently drawn from Ovid's *Metamorphoses* (Aeneas plucking the golden bough, his passport to the underworld; Perseus striking the sea-monster; Cadmus slaying the serpent of Mars; and a fourth scene too defective for certain interpretation). That such deeds of prowess were glossed by those who viewed them is rendered more likely by study of the largest floor at Frampton. In the centre is Bellerophon on Pegasus, slaying the Chimaera. The story might have been taken from Hyginus' *Genealogiae* but it was well-enough known from other sources. Three surrounding scenes (the fourth is lost) show the moon-goddess Selene and the eternally sleeping Endymion, Attis and Sangaritis and Creusa with Jason's children. The iconographic origin for the last might again lie in an illuminated copy of the *Metamorphoses*, the others respectively in the *Amores* and the *Fasti*. What is being contrasted is activity (*negotium*) against dalliance (*otium*), and by extension life against death. The four lines of verse in the border contrast Neptune with his dolphins, 'allotted the domain stirred by the winds' (i.e. the Ocean) with the ever active Cupid representing the young Bacchus who 'performs no service he does not deem fit' (*RIB* 2448.8). A completely separate floor at the end of a long corridor shows Neptune with his attendant winds.

The theme of Neptune as the ante-type of Bacchus, the sea thiasos contrasted with the land thiasos, has already been noted at Woodchester and Stonesfield. At Withington, Gloucestershire an Orpheus floor by Cirencester or Bath mosaicists had a panel depicting Neptune with his trident appended, at a later period, by a mosaicist from Dorchester. Evidently this connexion of themes was highly meaningful for the patron. Its most splendid manifestation in Britain, however, is not on a mosaic floor at all, but on the great silver dish from Mildenhall, Suffolk which has at its very centre a mask of Neptune with his dolphins, surrounded by a frieze of Nereids, itself encircled by the major frieze of Bacchus and his friends.

One anomalous, apparently jarring, element on the large Frampton mosaic is a recess on which the central motif is a cantharus; here it cannot be interpreted simply as a conventional Bacchic vessel, because the Christian emblem of the chi-rho is shown above it on the chord of the apse. This has to be considered alongside its appearance on a mosaic from another large complex, at Hinton St Mary, probably laid by the same mosaicists. As though to demonstrate this, one part of the floor has within a roundel Bellerophon and the Chimaera. Instead of the contrast of unhappy love scenes here the episode is flanked by panels of hounds chasing stags. Life is difficult and uncertain. The main panel has at its centre the bust of a clean-shaven youth with the chi-rho, in this case behind his head which is flanked by two pome-granates in the field. It is hard not to interpret this bust as that of Christ who, after his crucifixion, went down to Hades and liberated Adam. The pomegranates of course recall the myth of Demeter and Kore; they symbolise eternal life coming out of death. Three lunettes around the panel portray hounds chasing deer, again reminders of the pains of life, evoking the words of Psalm 22, verse 16:

'For dogs have compassed me: the assembly of the wicked have inclosed me: they pierced my hands and my feet.'

The fourth lunette contains a Tree of Life. This is a very ancient and widespread symbol but by the fourth century had largely become a Christian motif. A fine tree of life with a dove perched in its branches is shown on a gold ring found in Suffolk and now in the British Museum.

All the images at Hinton St Mary (apart from Bellerophon) would seem to be unequivocally Christian in nature, even the four figures in the spandrels which have lost their attributes (if they were ever meant to be Seasons) and might represent the four Evangelists. There does seem to be a difference in religious tone, though not in artistic style, between Hinton St Mary and Frampton. The former is no longer closely connected with the pagan world though the resolute programme of action looks towards the sort of Christianity out of which Pelagius' theology arose; at Frampton Christian symbol is still very much tied in to a classical ambience, as indeed it is at Lullingstone where as we have seen Christ's name is encoded in a verse alluding to the *Aeneid*. In like manner these mosaics show how a pagan myth (that of Bellerophon) could acquire Christianising overtones, or possibly (at Frampton anyway) how paganism could attempt to absorb Christianity.

The late Roman mosaics of Britain are unusual, not only for their eccentric and erudite iconography but also for their artistic style which is, for the most part, distinctly linear in the manner in which the subject matter is portrayed; this subject matter is largely mythological and eschews certain themes very popular elsewhere (notably beast fights and gladiators). Mythological scenes reflect the popularity of Ovid, Vergil and Hyginus as well, no doubt, of other authors. At Low Ham, Somerset, the floor of the bathhouse was ornamented with scenes from books two and four of the *Aeneid*, and perhaps the dining room at Lullingstone suggest the ownership of deluxe editions. Everywhere there is the influence of the schooling which nurtured a tightly organised society in which everyone knew everyone else. We see in Romano-British provincial society the same sorts of coterie which we glimpse through the pages of Macrobius' *Saturnalia*, where the author describes the highly cultivated winter festivities of pagan aristocrats near Rome. Such people would have felt equally at home in fourth-century Britain.

Unfortunately we have no record of the daily life of Julian's friend Alypius while he was in Britain. At the period when Julian was Caesar in Gaul, Alypius was Vicarius of the Britanniae and thus stationed in London, capital of Maxima Caesariensis. Later Julian's right-hand man in his restoration of pagan and traditional rites (such as Temple-based Judaism), Julian summoned him in the months prior to his revolt in 360 with the promise of 'hunting small deer'! His interests presumably did include hunting; but in reading Julian's prose poems, such as his praise of the Mother of the gods, we glimpse a late pagan faith entirely consistent with what Julian and his great friend might have known from Britain. This was friendly territory, united in its mistrust of the central power (as we shall see below) but also in its positive, active, religious ethos. The one political statement is the stone (*RIB 103*) recording the re-dedication of a column to Jupiter Best and Greatest in Cirencester at this time or a year or two later by Lucius Septimius, governor or *praeses* (*rector* is the poetic term used in the hexameters) of [Britannia] Prima:

> *Signum et erectam prisca religione columnam*
> *Septimius renovat primae provinciae rector*

47   *Gold coin of Julian, neo-Platonic philosopher and last of the great pagan emperors*

Despite attempts to date the inscription earlier, the name of the province Britannia Prima is post Diocletianic and the only period at which a pagan monument, perhaps deliberately thrown down, is likely to have been restored is under Julian. This inscription is, indeed, the latest surviving building inscription of Roman Britain.

The prosperity of the province and of its vibrant cultural life is also emphasised by extraordinary finds of treasure, mainly from East Anglia though it is virtually certain these finds would have been reflected in the treasures of the great villas of the south and south-west; indeed the Hoxne treasure is stylistically related to the forms of figural art in mosaic from Britannia Prima. It is not known how the Mildenhall treasure from Suffolk was used or who its final owner might have been, but the balance of opinion is beginning to view it in the context of a rich landowner rather than an official from elsewhere in the Empire. It is dishes such as this which would have been displayed in Woodchester and other great houses. Scenes on caskets in the Esquiline and Sevso Treasures show domestic toilet-silver being carried to the *domina*, and such ceremonial display must have been common in British villas. One significant find from the south-west is a hand-washing bowl, similar to an example in the Mildenhall Treasure, from a trial excavation at a probable villa-site at Blunsden Ridge, Wiltshire.

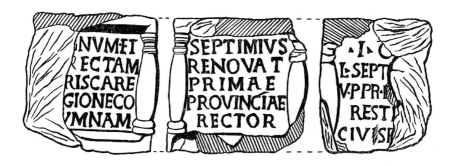

48   Inscription recording the re-erection of a Jupiter column at Cirencester in Julian's reign.
Drawing: Haverfield trustees

Two very important recent finds of treasure (both jewellery and plate) from East Anglia throw considerable light on the social and religious milieu of the upper classes of Roman Britain. The Hoxne treasure (Suffolk) contained a vast quantity of coin and jewellery as well as a number of smaller table vessels and spoons. A number of spoons are decorated with sea-creatures and dolphins and two strange spoon-strainers bear busts of Neptune, very much resembling the head on the Frampton pavement, accompanied in each example by a pair of dolphins. A prancing tigress, once the handle of a ewer, clearly evokes Bacchus. It is probable that many of the items were of British manufacture but unlikely that they have religious, or at least pagan significance, as several of the items in the Treasure bear Christian symbols, chi-rhos or crosses. One of the owners was a '*domina*', the Lady of the Estate, called Juliana; an open-work bracelet which evidently belonged to her carries a legend wishing her good luck. Chi-rhos shown on some items at Hoxne suggest the family may have been Christian. But how can we explain a body chain, with a jewelled amethyst and garnet centre-piece in front and an open-work setting containing a coin of Gratian behind? Venus wears just such a chain in one of the panels of the Low Ham pavement. The owners of the treasure carried their piety lightly, perhaps?

By contrast the Bacchic *thiasos* clearly did mean a very great deal to the aristocratic owners of the Thetford treasure (Norfolk). Many of the spoons in the treasure were dedicated to Faunus, a god from Latium mentioned by early Roman poets including Vergil and Ovid, but not heretofore known to be the subject of a sophisticated cult anywhere in the Empire. A satyr-like figure on a gold buckle suggests that Faunus was considered to be a god rather like Bacchus, and perhaps equated with him; and one of the two gilded spoons shows a panther (and another a triton, for the marine *thiasos*). Two rings have hoops composed of dolphins; another has woodpeckers drinking from a cantharus. The god was given various epithets such as 'Medigenus' meaning 'mead-begotten' and 'Ausecus' meaning 'prick-eared' like Pan. The worshippers of Faunus called themselves by names such as Ingenuus, Silviola and Agrestis which have rustic overtones but we do not know whether they were real names or *signa* (nick-names) used in cult.

49   *Mosaic from villa at Grateley, Hampshire with the central device of a fan*

Perhaps we might see the Hoxne Treasure as having originally been used in the context of a palatial *domus* such as the Woodchester villa. The life of such estates centred around hunting and farming for men, visiting and displaying one's jewellery, coiffure and toilet silver for women. A mosaic found at East Coker, Somerset, now in Taunton Museum shows two men carrying a deer on a pole. It is reminiscent of scenes on the Little Hunt mosaic at Piazza Armerina or, much closer to Britain, the famous hunting mosaic from Lillebonne in Northern Gaul. Hunting scenes, especially hare coursing, are common themes in art. A mosaic uncovered in the villa at Grateley, Hampshire depicted a fan – like the mirror, an attribute of Venus on the Kingscote mosaic, a vital accessory for the Roman woman. By contrast, the world of the Thetford Treasure is analogous with that at a private cult-centre like Littlecote. What binds them both together is the common culture of the Romano-British ruling class, a study of which suggests that the life of the privileged in provincial society was a happy one.

But outside the world of scholarly relaxation there were problems. These were very much concerned with relationships to the Roman government and in order to understand the tensions which led the privileged men and women of Roman Britain to revolt and to threaten their own material comfort we need to consider the political circumstances of the time. Freedom is, after all, the most precious possession human beings have, apart from life itself. The very culture the Britons so valued ultimately led them to reject what had come to seem to them a foreign and unfamiliar Empire in which Grace (*Gratia*) took precedence over Law.

50 Fashionable dining. Dido and Aeneas recline upon a stibadium. *The manuscript, the* Vergilius Romanus, *is very probably Romano British and is certainly true to the villa culture of the British 'Golden Age'.* Photo: courtesy Vatican Museums

May 405. A villa outside Corinium.

The Lady Juliana was sixteen years old, and preparations were in hand for her betrothal party arranged by her indulgent father Aurelius Ursicinus. Someone had told her that Ursicinus came from Ursus, a bear, 'Artos' in Celtic. He was a bear of a man and frightfully, frightfully rich. A great chest of coin was assembled as a dowry and all her friends had showered gifts on her including an exquisite bracelet given to her by her cousin, Valeria. *'Utere Felix Domina Iuliane'* it read. She was a real 'Lady' now.

51 *Gold ring from Thetford Treasure showing woodpeckers* (picus) *alluding to Faunus' father.* Photo: British Museum

All day, deer and hare, game-birds and fish had been brought in from outlying parts of the estate. The wedding feast would be sumptuous as befitted a member of one of the leading families of Corinium, the foremost family after that of the governor and he was only here for a few years at a time. Her family also owned estates near Bath and at Venta Belgarum, and the fleeces they produced were processed in the Imperial fulling mill there. Juliana had gone to church that morning – it was expected of her – but she preferred the colourful ceremonies that still went on at the country temples and even at Bath, where one could get one's fortune told and ask Mercury or Mars or Minerva to punish people one did not like. Lavinia had taken her gloves, horrid girl. She would curse her unless she brought them back. And she would curse that priest, Justus. Some people said that you could not curse Christians but she had been told you could add to the formula 'Whether man or woman, boy or girl, slave or free' the words 'pagan or Christian'.

She looked at the great circular floor of the hall and danced across it . . . in honour of Orpheus. That would show the boring old priest, who had told her to cut her hair, who was in charge here. A smile crept across her face. She would ask him . . . and make sure he was thoroughly shocked. The gold, jewelled body chain came out of its box. Her Nubian slave, Salome (she had chosen that name especially to annoy that

52 *Venus wearing a body chain, casting her spell on Dido and Aeneas. From Low Ham, Somerset, now in Taunton Museum.* Photo: Institute of Archaeology, Oxford

odious priest!) was ever so pretty, like a bronze statue which had acquired a rich brown patina, like an image of the goddess Venus in fact. And Salome was her best friend too!

It was night; the party was in full swing. The lady Juliana fanned herself with an expensive ivory fan. The bracelets, all three of them on her slender white forearm, jingled enticingly. Beautiful German page boys with long perfumed hair and neck-torques of white gold poured out glasses of ice-cold wine, just like they did for Dido in her father's very expensive and rare illuminated Vergil manuscript. She longed to touch the boys and run her hands down their locks and kiss them on their faces. They looked so much fresher than her podgy would-be husband, Gregorius, who came from Belgica. She would have to marry him, but she would have dear Salome with her so it would be alright.

The professional dancers had arrived; they enacted the 'Dance of the Four Seasons'. Then a young man performed an acrobatic and dramatic solo piece called 'The Triumph of Bacchus' at the end of which he was lifted high by the maenads and scattered rose petals over the guests. Finally she, as 'Mistress of the Feast', clapped her hands and Salome entered for an unexpected, unrehearsed finale. One by one Salome discarded her veils. Justus would get the allusion – and be scandalised. Good! Before long, and very much to the consternation of her indulgent and well-meaning father, Salome stood stark naked before the assembled company . . . apart from the jewelled body chain which

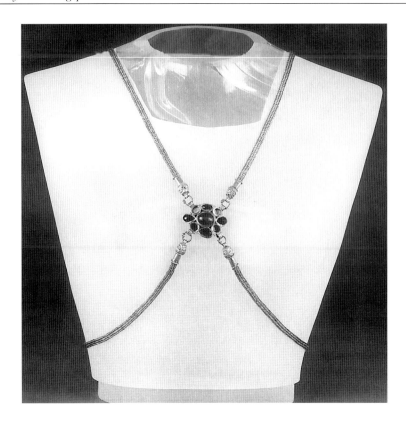

53 *Body chain from treasure found at Hoxne, Suffolk. As worn by Venus and by dancing girls.* Photo: British Museum

clung to her body and drew attention to her pert, fig-like breasts and her mound of Venus, as though she were in bondage or as though she were, indeed, the great goddess Venus herself. She pirouetted very seductively, to the ever more rhythmic clapping of the more drunken of the guests, who very much relished this extra entertainment. The goddess of love was certainly presiding over the revels this time.

'Cras amet qui nunquam amavit . . .'; Juliana sang the old song to herself sotte-voce. 'But where would the Roman province of Britannia Prima be, without the dance', she thought, 'the wild, self-indulgent dances of the Celts which had come down to her own time, were the same as they had always been, however classicised they now seemed to be. And was the Church to threaten even the refined Roman ballet?'. Then she reflected further: 'But the dance is not just a way of life to us Celts; it is inborn in human nature; it is a gift to mankind from the ancient gods who have seen everything. Such a dance as Salome had just danced was, after all, danced for Dido and her Aeneas in Carthage, long, long ago.' She had, she once again reminded herself, seen the paintings in her father's book. He would understand how she felt; he would forgive her. She rushed over, first to Salome and kissed her warmly, and then to her father and gave him a kiss as well. She did not kiss the priest!

7 The metamorphosis of
Roman Britain

December AD 409.

Aurelius Ursicinus had ridden hard from his villa in the land of the Dobunni through a landscape made dreary by the continual drizzle; the meeting was urgent and his presence was needed in Londinium. The civilians had pressed to have first Marcus and then Gratian made Emperor, though the remit of neither could extend further than Britain. The position on the nearer continent was chaotic. War and rebellion, especially rebellion, threatened everywhere. The army, or what called itself the army, composed of field divisions stationed mainly at the towns of the south wanted a military adventure and had deposed and killed Gratian, the unanimous choice of the curiales. Selecting Constantine, an illiterate adventurer who styled himself Constantine III, they had at last departed on a fleet of ships to ravage and make their fortunes on the continent.

Representatives from the cities of Britannia Prima - Marcus from Durnovaria; Paulinus from Calleva; Carinus from Noviomagus; Bonosus from Venta amongst them - sat together. Others came from elsewhere, especially the south-eastern province of Maxima Caesariensis, amongst them Avitus, representing Rochester, an old school friend of Aurelius who owned several estates in Kent including one at Lullingstone which he was giving to the church. A vote was taken. Each agreed to set up a new, quasi-Republican constitution in Britain, to live under their own Roman laws, even if nominally as clients of Honorius.

Avitus gave them a resumé of the recent history of Rome in Britain. He reminded them that our people had accepted Rome from the beginning, 'but', he told them 'it was always a contract; we were their clients and they were our patrons. Life has not been the same since Constantius I seized the island. Sure we have had great art and great wealth, or some of us have. Nevertheless, since his time and that of his unbalanced and violent son, we have had rebellion on my reckoning about every ten years. Only in the middle century did our own Magnentius offer a bit of relief . . . and what a price we had to pay at the hands of Constantius II's creature, Paul the Chain! Then we had the great and noble Julian, under whose mild rule we had superb governors, Alypius as Vicarius in Maxima and Lucius Septimius as Rector of Prima. You once showed me the great column of Jupiter which he re-erected in Corinium. My personal tribute to Jupiter was to lay the Europa and the Bull mosaic in my dining room - a Christian is, I suppose, allowed to have fun at the gods' expense - I cannot forget my education; I am an

54   Gold coin of Constantine III

Ausonius type of Christian. Do you like Ausonius' poems? A wonderful description of the villas on the Moselle. You should read it sometime . . . but I digress.

'In 367, came the "great uprising" which our enemies dismissed as a "barbarian conspiracy". It was a time to keep one's head low and to know nothing. But I did know Valentinus and rather agreed with his grievances. While we paid some Irish pirates and a few tribesmen from north of the Wall and a few Saxons to divert the useless soldiers we massed what forces we could raise on the plains of Wiltshire but that Count Theodosius, father of the fanatic emperor of that name, and his two unworthy sons, one of whom I suppose we should acknowledge out of form, until we have decided what to do, was just too strong for us. I was lucky not to lose my property and my life. This time there will be no mistake.'

In such fashion, over wine and seated in the half-ruined palace of the erstwhile Vicarius on the Eastern side of Londinium, was the new order proclaimed. Britain was Roman and not Roman; loyal and disloyal. Dimly, Aurelius realised that they had passed a watershed. He took out a coin from his purse. A newly minted siliqua of Constantine III. What would happen to the coinage? the towns? the villas? the old secure life?

'Three years ago I betrothed my daughter, Juliana, to Gregorius of Lillebonne. He had a big estate near there. The dowry was enormous and I had it packed in two trunks. Lady Juliana went with one of them, by sea from Chichester. She arrived safely and so did her trunk, quite a lot of silver and some expensive enough dresses. I sent the money, the smaller items of plate, and the jewellery – why does she need all those bracelets? – and Salome's body chain. Surely she wasn't planning another sex show? If she does, Salome will be totally starkers, because my men ran into a straggle of Constantine's army . . . they said they were off to join him . . . real desperados. The sort of people Britain is best without. Well Paulus and Ingenuus were surrounded in a wood which they perceived to be holy ground. They could either have met the soldiers, the dosh would have been taken and they would have been killed or they could bury it for the gods to keep, Faunus is said to be good at that . . . and make a sharpish get away. What would you have done? I am a fair man and trust old Ingenuus who saved my life from a falling tree once. I may be able to get the stuff back some day, if the chaps can remember the wood. Gregorius will just have to be content with what he has got.'

Carinus spoke up. 'Yes everyone is burying things. It is in the air or something. It does not take soldiers either; it is an old Celtic custom. Elsewhere there are temple treasuries. There is a custom amongst us Celts to toss all our possessions into a river or a lake. Think of all that gold Julius Caesar got out of a lake in Toulouse.'

'You have to be drunk to do such a silly thing!' exclaimed Bonosus.

'But we Celts are ALWAYS getting drunk', replied Marcus.

'Well, things can only get better?' Paulinus' platitude was half a question. Would they? Could they materially? Who would keep up the roads, the baths, the villas, the elaborate communications network, without money, without money . . .

'All I know', Aurelius thought, 'is that I must be true to myself, as King Verica, long ago was true to himself. The life of a man is divided into body and spirit; the one grows old and decays as the Roman state has decayed; but God (and he was tempted to use the plural for once) does not decay . . .'

Their favourite stories were all of metamorphosis, of men and women changing into other men and women, or into animals and plants. This shape-changing fancy, found in native myth and art as well as in the classical beauty of Ovid's verse, provides the backdrop to events after the officials of Imperial government were thrown out.

As seen in the past this was often viewed as a time of chaos, followed by bloody Anglo-Saxon conquest with the surviving Britons taking refuge in Wales, Dumnonia and Brittany. Apart from the fact that this model vastly belittles the importance of the British west, that triangle of cities, the old colonia of Gloucester, Cirencester and the spa of Bath remaining in British hands until AD 577, it is evident that the story of Germanic conquest owes a great deal to scenarios of more modern times. Archaeological and historical sources, though often very ambiguous, can be seen rather differently, often in fact through cultural change in which Romano-Celtic identities became Anglo-Saxon. Artistic tastes underwent rapid but logical change and many of the ruling class came to speak the language of Angles, Jutes and Saxons rather than Celtic or even Latin.

Some of the evidence for catastrophic decline in the infrastructure of daily life can be seen as inherent even in the 'golden age of Roman Britain', the fourth century. Then the public buildings of the towns fell into decay, rubbish lay in the theatre, the basilica became dangerous or collapsed, wealth accumulated in fewer and fewer hands. Other factors were the immediate consequence of the snapping of fiscal links with Rome. Yet other catastrophes did not happen or have been vastly exaggerated.

Britain was not overrun by savage hordes of barbarians. The northern frontier subsided into a series of fortified farms kept by onetime soldiers. The Birdoswald 'garrison', now of twenty '*limetanei*' herded sheep as though they had returned to the Roman pastoral idyll. The curiales of nearby Carlisle, capital of the Carvetii, took the opportunity to expand its territory across the Solway and south to Catterick at the behest of the small communities around about who felt that Carlisle men were 'efficient' guardians of the peace. Soon the chief magistrate of the Carvetii would declare himself ruler of a new kingdom, Rheged.

Connexions with the Central Empire remained tenuous. The story of the British civitates appealing to Honorius is almost certainly fictitious. Honorius could not even control Italy and the rescript acually told one of the communities of the south, Bruttium, to look to its own defense. The 'groans of the Britons to Aetius thrice consul' in the mid-century is probably another fabrication.

But if the Roman state was not in a position to show interest, the church was. Christianity was making headway because of its superb organisation, allowing it to act almost as a State within a State. One worry was that half cut off from the outside world the British church would go its own way without allegiance to Rome. A rather conservative British cleric called Pelagius had gone to Rome and preached doctrines about the importance of free will which he and many others thought entirely unexceptionable. The trouble was that he and his followers like Coelestius, another Briton, were out of date. The semi-Manichaean, Augustine of Hippo, was teaching that good works were nothing without the 'Grace' of God. The word was unfortunate: Grace meant 'favour', oiling the palms of officials in order to get access to governors or emperors, it stank of the dislocation of Emperor and Citizen. Pelagius' cry 'I cannot bear it' was a decisive moment. Pelagianism as such was expounded as a 'new' doctrine in Rome. In Britain it was normal and epitomised in Christian circles by the classical myth of Bellerophon's exploits, riding on Pegasus to slay the fire-breathing Chimaera.

It drew visitors to Britain, amongst them, in 429, Germanus. He went to Verulamium where he was met by the town magistrates resplendent in their robes of office. Here he promoted the cult of Alban, taking relics, a finger, part of Alban's supposed staff or some such items back to Auxerre. In fact as we have noted Alban may have been a supporter of Albinus (which could account for his name) who was put to death under Severus, or he could have been a supporter of Allectus. More intriguingly he could have been a smart Christianisation of the head-cult which had grown up around the grave of the king of the house of Cunobelin who had died and been buried with great ceremony around AD 55. During his visit Germanus had scattered some brigands with the shout of 'Alleluia'. Did he arrange this charade?

What the episode does show is the beginning of what looks like mass conversion to Christianity across Britain. It is especially marked in the west with early Christian gravestones of individuals, some with evocative names such as Carausius and Caratacus.

The stones are informative about native society. The names are Celtic or Latin. As they are the subject of several major studies, in recent years most notably by Professor Charles Thomas, only a small selection need be mentioned. A splendid memorial from Margam in South Glamorganshire is inscribed: *Bodvoc hic iacit / filius Catotigirni / pronepos Eternalis Vedomavus.* The name Bodvoc, that of a king of the Dobunni in the first half of the first century AD, was evidently still extant in the mid-sixth. His great grandfather who has a partially Latin name lived in the middle of the fifth century, no doubt, and may even have met people who remembered Magnus Maximus. In Penmachno, Caernarfonshire, is the famous memorial reading: *Carausius / hic iacit / in hoc con / geries la / pidum.* This has been shown by Charles Thomas to be an immensely subtle and moving epitaph in which the dedicator, with the Latin name Viola, encodes her name within the inscription. Although her name is not attested in Roman Britain, that of Carausius is of course that of the evidently popular late third-century ruler and the name reappears on coins of AD 354-8, perhaps hinting at an otherwise unrecorded attempt at rebellion against Constantius II. Another memorial stone is to be seen now built into the exterior south wall of the church at Llanfihangel Cwm Du in Brecknockshire. It reads: *Catacus hic Iacit / Filius Tegernacus*. Both names are Celtic; the beginning of a name beginning Cata... is scratched on a comb from Fishbourne, but the name also brings to mind that of the famous Caratacus. The father's name is thought to be Irish like that of Tigernaci on a stone from Jordanston in north-west Pembrokeshire, also inscribed in ogham. The absorption of an Irish element into the population was a widespread phenomenon, recorded as far east as Silchester where an ogham memorial gives the name of Tebicatos.

Most of the inscriptions belong to members of the ruling class, kings, princes and magistrates or to priests and other ecclesiastics. There is also the remarkable stele of a doctor whose father had the common late Roman name Martinus and who was evidently practising in north-west Wales: *Meli medici / fili Martini / i[a]cit*.

A few inscriptions add something about the organisation of society. Thus another tombstone from Penmachno, Caernarfonshire reads: *Cantori(x) hic iacit / [V]enedotis cive(s) fuit / [C]onsobrino(s) / Ma[g]li / magistrat*. Cantorix was a citizen of the state of Gwynedd (Venedos) and was the cousin of the magistrate called Maglos. Nor is this all, for in the same place another stone is dated by the consulate of Justus (AD 540); the dating is no doubt approximate for he was the last recorded consul but the stone displays a knowledge of a wider world: *fili Avitori / in tempo[re] Iusti[ni] con[sulis]*. Of course this was the period at which trade with the east Mediterranean was flourishing, as shown by the thriving entrepot at Tintagel, possibly the power-base of the king of Dumnonia.

The kingdoms of western Britain imported wine, oil and other commodities (represented by amphorae) as well as fine pottery from Asia Minor (Phocaean wares), the Levant and North Africa. Such pottery has been found at what were probably the sites of chieftains' courts at Cadbury Congresbury, South Cadbury, Dinas Powys and, of course, Tintagel. It has been found at Whithorn in south-western Scotland and even reached Ireland in small quantities (Dalkey, near Dublin). These commodities not only prove the consumptions of Mediterranean foods by the élite but also hint at Late Roman (Byzantine) styles of dining. With the comestibles there were surely many other objects including items of metalwork, gems and textiles. Whilst only a bronze censer from Glastonbury and a garnet intaglio, originally in a gold setting, depicting a scorpion from a settlement at Cefn Cwmwd, Anglesey have been found in the West, a great many other imported objects from the Byzantine Empire, gems, bronze vessels and even silver plate, are known from Eastern Britain (though some of these may have been imported to Kent from Merovingian Gaul). Although literary evidence such as that provided by Procopius shows that the Byzantines had an imperfect knowledge of Britain, there may have been some diplomatic activity with a Christian people which, in some sense, still considered itself to be Roman.

Evidence for the continuity of a culture both Roman and Celtic is different in nature and quality between western and eastern Britain. In the west (predominantly Wales, Devon, Cornwall and southern Scotland) there is historical evidence for the creation and survival of kingdoms, backed by some literary texts and a wealth of epigraphy. The latter is remarkable because the practice of erecting commemorative stones and even milestones had largely died out in Britain in the early fourth century and this was a revival. It is, indeed, more probable that the practice of erecting inscribed stones in Western Britain was reintroduced from Gaul late in the following century than that the practice hung on in Britain. The Septimius stone from Cirencester (*RIB* 103) in my opinion must date to around AD 360. Even later is a stone in much rougher capitals from one of the lighthouses narrowly spaced on the treacherous East Yorkshire coast. The Ravenscar inscription (*RIB* 721) read '*Iustinianus p(rae)p(ositus) / Vindicianus / magister turr[e]m (et) castrum fecit / a so(lo)*'. The late Phillip Bartholemew even speculated that this might be an early Christian stone, but the lettering does not really relate to these and a late fourth- or early fifth-century date seems more probable. It does however suggest a society in change with new, perhaps local titles, '*praepositus*' (if that is what the abbreviation 'pp' means) and '*magister*' presumably imply a first officer and a second officer just as at Lydney we have a '*praepositus religionis*' and an '*interpres*' (*RIB* 2448.3).

Society was in a state of flux from the very beginning of the fifth century if not earlier. A *praepositus* or a magistrate, the commander of a '*castrum*', a town or a district could become a ruler, a 'proud tyrant' (*superbus tyrannus*) in the words of Gildas (*De Excidio Britonum* 23 and 27) or in other words a king. In the mid-sixth century Gildas lambasted a number of them for their supposed moral failings. They were Constantine of Dumnonia, Aurelius Caninus, possibly ruling in Gloucestershire, Vortipor of the Demetae in south-west Wales, whose title on his memorial stone was in fact '*Protector*'; Cuneglasus, with a name means 'the grey hound', in Powys; and Maglocunus, 'the great hound', in Gwynedd in north-west Wales. Their names both Latin and British demonstrate the continuity of culture and it is not without interest that three (Caninus, Cuneglasus and Maglocunus) have a 'hound' element in their names: Maglocunus is in fact Cunomaglus, the Apollo of Nettleton, reversed.

Considering the strength of paganism even quite late in the Roman period, as revealed by the Thetford Treasure for instance, and despite evidence for conversion contained in the cryptic inscription discerned by Charles Thomas and myself on the Lullingstone mosaic, it is still highly remarkable that where religion is specified in the writings of Constantius of Lyons (on the Germanus mission), Patrick and Gildas, it is always Christianity. In his *Epistola* Patrick admonishes the backsliding, slave-trading Coroticus, and Gildas lambasts contemporary kings – but for sinfulness, not paganism. He writes of the old pagan religion in the past tense: 'I shall not list the diabolical monstrosities . . . some of which we can see today, inside and outside deserted cities, their features deformed and ugly as ever' (Gildas, *De Excid. Brit.* 4, 2-3). Symbols on fifth-century memorials from Wales, when they occur, are inevitably Christian too, chi-rhos and crosses.

The evidence of Constantius' life is especially telling for in 429 he writes of St Germanus meeting a well-organised town council at Verulamium (not specified, but what other town is there near the shrine of Alban?). The enemy appears to be Pelagianism. This, the doctrine of Pelagius and his followers, is sometimes described as a 'heresy' but in fact it was not; it merely asserted the old-fashioned Christian view that we are the masters of our fate, and it seems to have continued to be expounded in Britain.

It has been suggested by Ken Dark and others that the religious change was the result of a social revolution from below, perhaps a Bagaudic uprising as in Western Gaul. I think such radical dislocation is unlikely. There is strong survival of the educational system which the writings of Patrick and Gildas demonstrate, and continued pride in *Romanitas* amongst the ruling classes, men such as Aurelius Ambrosianus, the victor of Mons Badonicus in *c.*AD 500 (Gildas, *De Excid. Brit.* 25,3). We are told that his parents before him had 'worn the purple' (*purpura*) though they had been killed in disturbances consequent on the revolt of the Saxon mercenaries.

It is more likely that the church, which had made considerable headway in some towns such as Dorchester in Dorset and clearly had a foothold in others, was quickly perceived as the one organisation which had kept the same sort of supra-national organisation as the Roman Empire. Men and women like Avitus of Lullingstone and Publianus, Amcilla, Innocentia and Viventia at Water Newton or Senicianus at Silchester could simply slide across from one religio-cultural belief system to another, just as could a cultivated poet like Ausonius in Gaul. Some of them may have continued to pray to the old gods; why else would Senicianus have the name of the goddess Venus on his ring; why else would Avitus display one of the more notorious loves of Jove and write a poem about it on a mosaic; why would he, together with the owners of the Hinton St Mary and Frampton villas, show the hero Bellerophon? We see this 'conversion' as a one-way ticket to monotheism, but it is not clear they regarded it quite in that light.

Evidence for the coming of the 'Saxons' has long been disputed. If Gildas can be relied upon, there would seem to have been a revolt of 'Saxon' mercenaries in the employ of the 'proud tyrant', whom the eighth-century Northumbrian writer Bede calls 'Vortigern' (*H.E.* 14-15). The account is highly simplified and the newcomers who in some cases had been in Britain for far longer than Bede suggests contained other settlers apart from the Angles, Saxons and Jutes mentioned by Bede. There were certainly Franks. It may be wrong to see the disturbances as racial any more than were the events of 367, but clearly anarchic times are not good for culture. Some communities appear to have decamped to Armorica – 'Little Britain', Brittany – with their priests, but there is no real evidence in the literature or in the archaeology for anything like genocide. It must always be remembered that Gildas, like Bede who followed him, was writing theological tracts. They differed in that for Gildas the Britons are the children of Israel, lashed by God for their sins, pride, avarice, sodomy and fornication. For Bede it is the English who are the chosen people.

Particular interest attaches to a people who appear in central southern Britain and the Middle Thames, admittedly a century later in the sixth century. The Gewissae (whose name means 'the reliable ones' in Anglo-Saxon) appear in Bede and in the later *Anglo-Saxon Chronicle* and West Saxon regnal lists. The founder of the house was Cerdic, perhaps appearing in the 530s. His name is a corruption of the Celtic Caradoc. One of his successors was called Ceawlin and another Cenwalh, both implying British origin. One important entry in the *Anglo-Saxon Chronicle* alludes to a battle at Dyrham in AD 577 and the capture of Gloucester, Bath and Cirencester

55   Enamelled penannular brooch found at Bath, diameter 7cm.
Photo: Institute of Archaeology, Oxford

from the British. These cities were beyond Cerdic's area of influence, in the
Hwiccian rather than the Gewissian area, as Nennius writing in the ninth century
tells us with regard to Bath, but their 'conquest' reflects the way in which mercenary
groups of Germanic or mixed Celtic-Germanic ethnic origin brought about cultural
shifts in terms of language and material culture. For the ninth-century compiler of
the *Chronicle* the 'events' of 577 marked a significant episode in the formation of a
state, but at the time in the mid-sixth century, they may not have been nearly as
decisive in relations between different groups.

The material evidence from south-central and eastern Britain is in some ways less
satisfactory than that from the Wales and Dumnonia, because of the absence of inscriptions. From 'Anglo-Saxon' cemeteries a great deal of metalwork has been found. The
earlier examples are matched in late Roman contexts. Chip-carved, abstract design and
simplified animal forms are found on brooches (the art is sometimes called 'quoit-
brooch-style' after one type of circular fibula), belt buckles, finger-rings and nail-
cleaners. The forms are late Roman and the origins of this abstract ornament are
clearly present in the late fourth century and can be seen in the friezes of somewhat
stylised animals around some of the Hoxne bracelets, as well as in the formal open-
work designs from the same treasure. Later metalwork has often been regarded as more
'Germanic', but throughout we are basically dealing with a portable art analogous to
that found elsewhere in Western Europe and even in the Mediterranean world. Belts
and brooches were pre-eminent symbols of rank in the Late Roman world and it is not

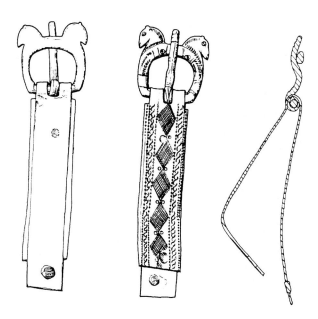

56 *Bronze zoomorphic belt buckle and plate from Houghton Down, Stockbridge, Hampshire, length 10cm.* Drawn by Alison Wilkins, Institute of Archaeology, Oxford

surprising that they were such important media for ornament.

What is missing from Britain as a whole are the glittering mosaics of the new churches in Rome, Ravenna or even central and Southern Gaul (as attested by Sidonius Apollinaris). The reason is quite simple. The monetary economy really had come to an end, though coins still seem to have been hoarded. The same absence of Mediterranean-style churches is apparent in the West, beyond any evidence for 'Anglo-Saxon' settlement. In Eastern Britain the epigraphic habit had either not been reintroduced or the inscriptions have not survived; (it is salutary to remember that outside the larger cities like London, Chichester and Cirencester, Roman inscribed monuments of the first to the fourth centuries are far from numerous). But in the fifth and sixth centuries there were, nevertheless, large Christian communities as there were in Western Britain, attested by cemeteries around the church in the Forum area at St Paul in the Bail, Lincoln, at St Albans, at Dorchester (Dorcic) in Oxfordshire (at Queenford Farm), and in the Chichester region notably at Highdown near Worthing. Their continuing Roman nature can sometimes be shown through their material culture. For example a coin and jewellery hoard at Patching near Highdown even contains late fifth-century issues, the last emperor attested being Libius Severus. Such caches as this or the Amesbury hoard with its curious and beautiful silver 'quoit-brooch-style' rings are generally regarded as bullion but possibly, as in late prehistory, they represent offerings, clearly now Christian in nature and representing the deliberate destruction of wealth. The Christian, Romano-Celtic speaking society of this area is less visible because it was not generally the custom here to bury grave-goods

*57   Silver rings from a hoard found at
Amesbury, Wiltshire. Bezels 10mm*

with the dead.

A few Christian objects do appear, however, notably the stoup depicting three biblical scenes from Little Wittenham, previously dismissed as a curiosity brought from Frankish lands, but now recognised as a native work demonstrating continuing artistic vitality amongst local Christians. In the centre is the baptism of Christ by Iohannes, whose name is boldly inscribed (see Matthew 3; 13-17). On either side are two other episodes, the miracle of the Marriage of Cana (John 2:1-10) and the tax collector Zacchaeus who has climbed a tree the better to see Jesus (Luke 19: 1-10). There is a large saltire cross within a circular frame on the other side of the vessel. The tradition of displaying such Biblical scenes is to be found much earlier, probably in the mid-fourth century in sheeting from a casket evenly folded over and 'killed' prior to dedication to the god Mercury at Uley. Here Christ and the centurion, Christ healing the blind man, Jonah reclining below a gourd and the sacrifice of Isaac were all depicted.

Even finer examples of sixth-century metalwork are the distinctive, insular 'Celtic' hanging bowls which first appear at this time. They are splendidly crafted with enamelled escutcheons generally of curvilinear style. Examples have been found for example in a rich burial at Lowbury Hill in Oxfordshire (which also contained an enamelled iron spearhead), and at Oliver's Battery, Winchester; but the finest come from the great royal burial at Sutton Hoo, Suffolk far to the east. Three mounts from a lost hanging bowl from the Anglo-Saxon cemetery at Faversham, Kent are of particular interest because in place of the usual enamelled trumpet-scrolls these mounts display open-work Latin crosses of regular Late Antique form though, flanked by dolphins of local appearance. These may date from late in the series, and were possibly influenced by Byzantine metalwork (as suggested in the following chapter). It is not known where the workshops for these bowls were located, but they may well have been within lands under the suzerainty of 'Anglo-Saxon' kings, and plausibly they could have been manufactured in Wessex. Earlier late-Roman enamelled metalwork from the region includes a very fine bronze pennanular brooch from the spring at Bath with enamelled terminals figuring two birds and a fish, and from Gloucestershire a silver hand-pin with

58   Bronze ring from Barton Court Farm, Abingdon. Diameter 25mm.
Photo: Oxfordshire Museums

enamelled ring.

Just occasionally, in studying the material evidence, we can see below the somewhat uniform accounts in the surviving, Christian literary sources to the persistence of a pre-Christian society. There is, for instance, a fine glass bowl deposited in a well at Pagans Hill, Somerset; the site of the temple at Woodeaton became known in Anglo-Saxon as *Harrowdonehill* suggesting continued use as a holy place (the memory of the Nemet is still recalled by the old parish name), and at Nymsfield, Gloucestershire where the Uley temple stands. In the late Roman cemetery at Highdown the custom of depositing grave goods persisted. Later, from the seventh-century 'Gewissian' cemetery at Winnal the rite of decapitating some corpses in order to free the spirit, a feature of local Roman pagan practice, was still observed. This admixture of Christianity with native paganism is something we would expect from any study of the literary evidence from Gaul, for instance in the writings of Gregory of Tours who records the veneration of Cybele still taking place annually in the countryside around Autun. In degraded form such echoes of the pagan past became an element in witchcraft.

4 June AD 500.

Aurelius Ambrosianus sat on his snow-white horse. The enemy had been scattered. To the east lay the land of another White Horse, hundreds of years old. He had ridden past it and made a wish, standing on the horse's eye. The Empire had been restored. The old books told him that Hadrian and Severus had built a wall as a bulwark against the barbarians – a mark of victory. There was still time before the harvest. He would ask his victorious soldiers to dig a great dyke (the Wansdyke) as his eternal monument, 'separating the Romans from the barbarians'.

Already he was being saluted in Latin as '*imperator*' and '*victor*', but a contingent from the dark lands of the Forest of Dean took up another title 'Artos! Artos! Artos!',

59   The walls of Caerwent, Gwent. A Roman city and early Christian holy site

the Great Bear, strongest of all the animals of Britain. So, he was to be the ante-type of 'Vortigern', the 'proud tyrant' who had started the trouble. As a noble and Christian king he would order his people to sing hymns as they undertook the work . . . but he could not help smiling at the stories his old nurse from Dorcic had told him about Dea Artio, the bear goddess, the Celtic Artemis, and hadn't he read in a book in the library of his schoolmaster-priest Paternus, that the only people who called themselves 'bears' in ancient Athens were little girls . . .

8 The gates of Dorcic

AD 601. Canterbury.

'Why did we ever come to this place?' Augustine mused aloud on the events of the past few years. 'It was a long and fearsome journey. Procopius, that old Greek scallywag, had heard from merchants about the Isle of Thanet and concluded it was the abode of Thanatos! Every night boats set out for Brittia. Although they appeared to be empty they were very low in the water as they sailed west, but they were as light as corks when they returned the following day. That was stupid, of course, but it did make you wonder. The old Roman historians were not too reassuring either . . . Britain was beyond Ocean, constantly raining and packed with hairy barbarians who sacrificed each other. At least the rain was true. Still a Christian should know how to cope with the desert, whether it was a wet desert or a dry one, and there were all those barbarians to convert, weren't there? Pope Gregory had said there were . . .

'And what did we find?' The future saint fixed Abbott Mellitus, who had been silently listening to his diatribe, with a fierce stare that was not very saintly. 'The place was positively swarming with Christians, who seemed to owe their loyalty to one Welsh saint or another. Furthermore they asked lots of questions . . . Somebody must have put them up to it! What was our view of one passage or another in Leviticus, about diet, about purity?'

'Surely you could answer them?'; Mellitus was conciliatory.

'Like Hell I could!' Augustine blushed with embarrassment. What had he just said? 'I almost replied that Leviticus was for Jews; but the fact remains the book is still part of our scriptures. God presumably intended it to mean something! So I wrote to the Pope. Gregory, bless him, got us into this mess, and he could get us out of it. But that was not the worst part . . .'

'What could be worse?' Mellitus considered the possibilities. 'A lot of local know-alls cause problems. I know the type of chap, stubborn in heresy. Some Pelagian behind them I expect, if they have such people still?'

Augustine shook his head and mopped his brow. 'No, it isn't really heresy; nothing we could really make stick as heresy. The worst part of the business is actually that they are very much better educated than us, they have read more books; they speak the clearest, cleverest Latin I have ever heard and spin little rings around us all the time with verbal tricks, double meanings and passages where you count the letters and find a sentence that contradicts what you thought the passage said. Now we have upset their bishops who have made it clear we are not very welcome here.'

'But the Anglo-Saxon kings? Surely they hold the political power in this part of the island?'

'Oh yes; they tolerate us. They like the glitter of the gold, the gems, the manuscripts and the very idea of Rome. They want to live and dress like Roman Emperors too. I can tell you that it is all a matter of authority. The Pope just wanted to add some ancient dioceses to his list. Britain was another province for the Universal Church to control. In fact he thinks just like one of those ancient emperors. Well at least if we can get a bit of cash from Ethelbert we can build some decent looking churches. This lot may speak pretty Latin but, all the same, their idea of a church is a wooden barn!'

Bede, although writing over a hundred years later and in northern Britain, does provide a reasonable historical account of the Augustinian mission and its aftermath. Although on the surface the aim was to convert the heathen, clearly the situation was not as simple as that. British Christianity was highly active, and in Canterbury King Ethelbert's wife was a Frankish princess called Bertha whose chaplain, Bishop Liudhard, had organised worship at 'an old church, built to honour St Martin in Roman times' (*Hist. Ec.* I.26). He founded or, as Bede tells us, repaired a church 'built long ago by Roman Christians' dedicated to Christ (I.33). This was an intramural church, now the cathedral.

It has to be said that archaeology has not established beyond doubt that there had been continuity of worship at either of these foundations or at other churches in the region from Roman times but there is a strong supposition that there was. At both Stone by Faversham and St Martin's, Canterbury, parts of the structure of the early 'Anglo-Saxon' churches are apparently Roman; but were they abandoned mausolea or long-functioning centres of Christianity?

Further west a meeting was arranged with some of the British bishops, perhaps in Oxfordshire at a place later called Augustine's Oak situated on the border between the territory of the Hwicce (perhaps representing part of the former Dobunni, a mixed British and 'Anglo-Saxon' group, no doubt) and the Gewissae. One recalls possible border meetings at temple sites like Frilford and Woodeaton in the events of AD 43. The Augustinian conference in 603 was similarly momentous in its consequences (*HE* II.2)

Not unnaturally the Britons were disinclined to give up age-old customs, such as their traditional date for Easter or their distinctive tonsures at the behest of a foreign emissary. At a second meeting, which may have been held at Aust where today the first Severn crossing takes the traveller over the river to Chepstow and South Wales, seven British bishops came to Augustine, intending to be conciliatory if he treated them as equals. However, as he remained seated in his chair and ordered their compliance, they went home.

This chapter is not concerned with the controversy between the Roman and Celtic churches as such. The doctrinal differences were not very great and renewed contacts with Rome would eventually lead to reconciliation and acceptance. These events do establish that the 'conversion' was more a political than a 'moral' event, and

60 *Beaker with Christian monogram and*
    Christian scenes, the Baptism,
    Marriage at Cana and Christ and
    Zacchaeus, from a grave at
    Wittenham, Oxfordshire, height 15cm

the tough questions on Judeo-Christian law which Augustine had to fire off to Pope Gregory (*H.E.* I.27) demonstrate the theological strength of his British critics. As David Howlett has demonstrated, they were better Latinists too.

What the mission could bring was a re-infusion of Mediterranean material culture. At the time of the political and cultural break between Britain and Rome in the late fourth and early fifth century, splendid churches were being erected in Rome, Ravenna, Milan, Naples and elsewhere, their walls and apses sparkling with mosaics in gold, red, blue and green. It is possible that London had a church based in its plan on St Thecla, Milan and it may have had marble veneered walls although only fragments remain. The painted walls of the Lullingstone house church provide a modest version of the jewelled magnificence of southern churches. It is possible that the Hinton St Mary mosaic with its bust of Christ was based on a design intended, in the first instance, for a vault.

Early British Christianity is attested throughout the island, but Roman-period churches are not and even the well-known 'church' at Silchester may be nothing of the sort. If it is a church it is very small and poorly furnished for an urban basilica, though a simple floor mosaic in the apse shows it did not totally lack pretention. Another still Roman early church is attested by a font at Richborough, Kent. In the fifth or sixth century St Paul in the Bail at Lincoln – with its burials which date it to a time when urban laws excluding burials from town had been abandoned – and the whitewashed monastic church (*Candida Casa*) of Nynia at Whithorn in Galloway

61 Enamelled discs in Celtic style from Chesterton-on-Fosse, Warwickshire. Diameters 65 and 53mm

again point to extreme simplicity. For all the texts and inscribed stones appertaining to Wales and the West, material evidence is scant.

While Anglo-Saxon church archaeology has not given us a S. Vitale or a S. Apollinare in Classe, and most of the more substantial buildings are now merely ruins or foundations, the visitor to the small Essex church of St Peter at Bradwell-on-Sea dated to 653, the ruins of SS Peter and Paul church at Canterbury, the church at Reculver, or even the later surviving churches in Mercia (at Deerhurst, Gloucestershire, Brixworth, Northamptonshire and Wing in Buckinghamshire), is aware that these buildings were, and still are, effectively Roman in texture and architectural style. Unfortunately what we cannot recover from archaeology is the effect of the paintings on the walls, the iconostasis, precious ivories and goldwork, though the sixth-century St Augustine's Gospels still preserved at Corpus Christi College, Cambridge do hint at the Late Antique magnificence we have lost.

Although it would have been possible for masons to model the earliest 'Anglo-Saxon' churches on remaining Romano-British exempla this seems not to have happened, at least in the south, and the main influences appear to have come from Northern Italy and Gaul. Eric Fernie suggests one reason for this may have been the hostility between the indigenous 'Celtic' church and the incoming 'Romans' at the time of the mission. The grandest example of the new Roman church existed up to the early nineteenth century at Reculver. Its demolition is perhaps the most grievous loss to our early historic heritage in that not-very-careful century. There was before the altar a triple arcade providing a place for a screen, curtains or even an iconostasis. Fortunately the columns remain, in the crypt at Canterbury Cathedral, sad relics of a noble church. The late Dr Thomas Blagg studied them and concluded that the carving of bases and capitals was, indeed, not in the Roman-British tradition of architectural sculpture.

In Wessex itself the Old Minster at Winchester, founded by Cenwealh in 648, was a large building evidently constructed of cut stone, a coronation church, closely associated with the palace. In appearance it might have had something in common with the chapel of St Lawrence which became the Mausoleum of Galla Placidia at Ravenna.

*62 Hanging bowl
     from Wilton,
     Wiltshire.
     Diameter 28cm*

Nothing is known of St Birinus' foundations at Dorchester, where he is said to have founded several churches (Bede, *H.E.* III.7) around 635. He was an Italian who had been sent to Britain by Pope Honorius I, after consecration by Asterius, bishop of Genoa, and is very likely to have built in an Italian manner. One of his foundations may have been in the town but another was very likely on an extra-mural site outside the East gate on the site of the later Abbey. If so, here at least, he may have been taking over a pre-existing church and a functioning church. Churches outside Roman towns were situated (as at St Albans) on cemetery sites where the bones of the martyrs or simply Christians held in reverence were venerated. The Abbey site is in just such a location. As noted above, at Dorchester (Dorcic) a cemetery has been excavated which points to Christian burial down to the sixth century, and the logical reason the kings Cynegils and Oswald gave Dorchester to Birinus was that it was a Romano-Christian town, suitable as a power base. Birinus died at Dorchester and was buried here, though his body was later translated to Winchester.

The material culture of the early seventh century reflects a world in which Christianity, Celtic and Roman, co-existed with Anglo-Saxon paganism. Even Christians were not averse to taking some of their 'treasures on earth' with them to the other world. The jewellery was very eye-catching, especially the masterpieces made in Kent; but examples of the spectacular gold and garnet cloisonné metalwork have been found further west, for example at Milton near Sutton Courtenay, Oxfordshire where composite brooches were found in two female graves, while a pyramidal fitting, possibly East Anglian, comes from Birinus' Dorchester. The mixed traditions of Wessex are revealed by a mount on a bag from a woman's grave at Swallowcliffe Down, Wiltshire whose mount divided into cloisons with a central jewel owes a great deal to the Kentish tradition though the stamped gold mounts which ornament it alternate 'Germanic' and Celtic designs. The use of large garnet beads on necklaces, for example by women buried at Winnal, Hampshire, or the use of gem-set pendants like a garnet cameo in a gold mount from Epsom, Surrey, show the strong desire to emulate current Roman (Byzantine) fashions.

Fashions in metal vessels were also changing. Although British Hanging bowls continued to be popular, there are examples from Faversham, Kent where the enamel

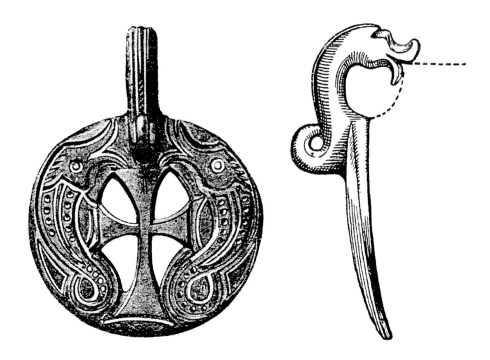

63   Escutcheon of hanging bowl from Faversham, Kent showing Byzantine influence. Diameter 50mm

escutcheons have been replaced by mounts with open-work long crosses in the centre, in Byzantine style. Alongside such native products there were also imported bronzes from the Eastern Roman Empire including a cast bronze bowl from the princely grave of a man buried with his horse under a barrow at Asthall, Oxfordshire. A probably royal grave, to judge from the number and richness of the grave goods which include gold clasps as well as an imported 'Coptic' bowl, was excavated from under a barrow at Taplow, Buckinghamshire. An ewer comes from Wheathamstead, Hertfordshire. A grave in the cemetery at Chessel Down on the Isle of Wight contained a bucket embellished with an engraved beast fight, with huntsmen confronting griffins and lions, clearly in the same tradition as earlier Roman hunting-vessels; an analogous vessel from a Mediterranean context depicts Achilles. One of the largest bronze bowls is of course that from Sutton Hoo, Suffolk which also contained a very impressive service of silver plate. The only example of early Byzantine bronzework from Western Britain is the censer found at Glastonbury, presumably used in the church there, and this has led to the general belief that all these exotic objects were brought to Britain from the nearer continent, but we should not forget the long established shipping routes to western ports and it is quite possible that some at least of these bronzes and other objects were traded in Britain from west to east.

Times were changing in other ways. A few Byzantine weights also reached England. Those from a grave at Watchfield, Oxfordshire were associated with a

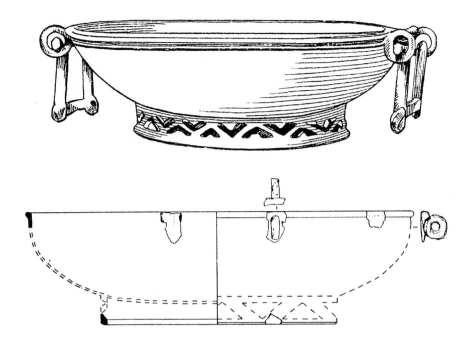

*64   Byzantine ('Coptic') bowl from Faversham, Kent, Diameter: 24cm and (below) a more
fragmentary example from the Asthall barrow, Oxfordshire*

balance and a selection of old coins including issues from the Greek East and from
near Taunton. The clearest testimony that Britain was once again becoming part of
a common culture was the re-introduction of coinage and the establishment of
trading *wics*, including Hamwic at Southampton, and Lundonwic along the Strand
and in the area of Aldwych, London. The designs on these early (seventh-century)
coins are based on late Roman issues, probably deliberately evoking the world of the
south in the same way that the Celtic kings had done six centuries before.

Dorcic. May 635.

On a flower-rich hay-meadow, near the banks of the river Thame, the townsmen
dressed in white or in bright colours waited patiently for the bishop to arrive. The
scene was reminiscent of that which had confronted Germanus two hundred years
before near Verulamium, as he came to pay his respects to the saint. The low fortifications of Dorcic, symbolic of the high status of the place, were hung with
bunting. Some said the name meant 'fort or walled town', but if so that probably
referred to the old British earthwork outside. 'No', thought Maelgwn as the chanting
of the Psalm began, 'not "fort" from *duro* but "eye" from *derc*; that would mean
"bright" or "splendid".'

143

The old gates were thrown open and a procession led by the kings, Birinus, the bishop, and the men from Rome passed through to take possession of Dorcic, now to be elevated to the rank of a cathedral city with a grand new church; though for the natives the most sacred place of the town would always remain the 'martyrium' beyond the East gate.

'In any case', Maelgwn concluded, 'it is bright and splendid enough now!'

If they had preserved any annals, did the Britons assembled there reflect that over half a millennium had passed since the aged King Verica had welcomed Aulus Plautius and the future emperor Vespasian to Britain? Here, on the frontier of Atrebates and Catuvellauni, in what was once a *mansio* for the Imperial Post where Marcus Varius Severus had set up his altar to Jupiter; here in the small, bustling town in Britannia Prima; here in the place where Britons and Gewissae (themselves half-British) had lived for so long side by side; the Christian inhabitants, the majority community, who had for centuries buried their dead within sight of this church welcomed the papal emissary as bishop.

65   *Lock plate from Dorchester, Oxfordshire in the form of a Janus head*

On the surface the contrast between the four-legion-strong invading army of 43 and the band of clerics who entered Dorcic on this day could not have been greater, but in reality there was considerable resemblance. In 43 the balance of power between the tribes in Britain had been broken and the Romans feared a hostile confederacy; now the success of an independent, predominantly monastic British church amongst Britons and Anglo-Saxons posed an enormous challenge to ecclesiastical discipline. There were tensions. The priest, Maelgwn, wondered how he would get on with these new Italian ideas. When Birinus had spoken to him he could hardly understand his Italianate Latin. Next year there was bound to be a fight over Easter. Maybe they would settle it by celebrating at different dates: Birinus in the town church and he in the church outside. But this could hardly work for long. The kings would not like it. They would have to decide it in a few years. He was old. It did not matter to him. There was a lot to be said for unity as in the days of Imperial Rome.

He was carrying a little offering box to raise alms for the poor. They had such things now that people again used coinage. It had a lock and he glanced down at the lock-plate. It was in the form of a Janus head, heads looking in opposite directions. The old Roman god of beginnings and endings, of the past and the future. 'It represents Rome past and Rome future', he thought. Then he laughed as he noticed that both heads had long, flowing Gewissean beards.

Postscript: Fairest Isle

Winchester; the Royal Palace.
22 March AD 893. Evening.

The king sat in his study, reading as he liked to do at this time of day. He followed the text of Vergil deftly with an ivory pointer, at the other end of which was a crystal jewel of ancient Roman workmanship. The crystal was antique, a gift from the Pope and enormously valuable; but behind the crystal was an exquisite image in cloisonné enamel of English workmanship showing a personification of sight. The gold openwork around the jewel was cut out to form the words *Aelfred mech acht gewyrcan* – 'Alfred caused me to be made'. The language, too, was English. Perhaps, he thought, he should translate the *Aeneid* for his subjects because it was such a wonderful tale of Imperial destiny and of hairbreadth escape from danger, and it fitted so well with his own story. Wasn't he, after all, a consul of the Romans? Hadn't the Pope solemnly clad him in the consular robes when he was only a little child? His thoughts turned to the great events of the Roman past, to Hannibal, to the invasions of the Cimbri and Teutones, the exploits of Julius Caesar and of the other Caesars who followed him. Then he thought back to the wars of the Greeks and of the wave upon wave of Persians who had crossed the Hellespont and ravaged Greece. It was said that their arrows were fired in such a dense cloud that they darkened the air; the Greek response to this was 'Then we will fight in the shade!'

How often in his little realm of Wessex, ringed by a circle of strong forts, a 'ring of steel' from Osnaforda and Wallingford in the north to Wareham and Portchester in the south, had he resisted the powerful army of pagan barbarians, and prevailed against all the odds. He was no Alexander, no Caesar. He had founded no vast Empire, and his interests were quite other than theirs. He had just done his duty to God and protected his people.

His friend, Guinn, the Welshman who had taken the Hebrew name Asser, 'blessedness', named after the eighth son of Jacob, from St Jerome, came into the king's chamber to wish him goodnight.

'Tell me', said the king, 'what do your Celtic traditions tell you about the just ruler?'

Asser replied slowly, 'My Lord King, remember that they are also your own traditions. Are you not descended from that Caradoc whom the English pronounce Cerdic who led the Gewissae? In Wales the "West Saxons" are, indeed, still called the Gewissae in token of their trustworthiness. Englishmen, Welshmen, Romans – we are all the same under God in your kingdom. The qualities of a great king are not the same as those of the mighty conqueror which some, wrongly, account worthy of the epithet "great".

66   *The Alfred Jewel,*
     obverse and reverse.
     Length 6cm

'Our ancient history tells of a boy who went to Rome as you went to Rome when he was very young. He became friends with Claudius who later became Emperor as you became friendly with the Pope. Allied with Claudius, that most unmilitary of Emperors, he rescued and restored his people, the Atrebates and their allies. He brought them culture just as you brought them culture, taught them to enjoy the classics; your translation of Pope Gregory's "Pastoral Care" is a far greater monument than all your military prowess. What did Xerxes leave or Alexander or Julius Caesar? Only widows. Their memory is without love, without blessing, without sanctification. Tiberius Claudius Togidubnus, heir to Verica was Great King, High King if you like, of extensive lands, the southern parts of which were for a long time known as the "Regnum". Later this became the most cultivated province of Britain, Britannia Prima and later still in your language it is Wessex. You, too, through blood and your good works are heir to Verica. Britain has had many rulers but not since our Togidubnus until you became king has any been called "great". Like Togidubnus you have founded cities with fair grids of streets in the Roman manner and dedicated them. I remember the simple, graceful stone which I saw at Shaftesbury; there is no bombast in the wording and greater stress on Our Lord than on yourself: *Aelfred Rex Hanc Urbem Fecit Anno Dominicae Incarnationis DCCCLXXX Regni Sui VIII.* You and Togidubnus have both lived your lives with compassion and sensitivity to others, sharing that quality the old Romans called "*humanitas*". My Lord, your learning has lifted you far above all the kings of Christendom and, even more than your ancestor (who was, after all, a pagan), you richly deserve the designation, "great".'

'My dear friend', Arthur replied, 'I owe all of this, my realm, my life, even that little wisdom I possess to Almighty God. I cannot see far into the future and whether we will always prevail against the relentless barbarian Northmen, as one "Great Army" follows another to pillage and loot, I do not know. But I will always believe that it is not through victories won with the sword alone that our peoples will ever achieve real victory, but through cherishing our sacred culture tenaciously, at whatever the cost, and being true to God through all the ages to come.'

'That is the true wisdom of a philosopher king', agreed Asser. 'I was just thinking of that wonderful poem, *The Ruin*, which is of course an English version of a Roman elegy about the mutability of all earthly power. As it happens it is about Bath and the decaying monuments of King Togidubnus. Let me quote a little of it:

> "Wonderful are these walls; though broken by fate . . . the roofs have fallen; the towers are in ruins. The grasp of the earth; the strong grip of the ground, holds the mighty builder . . . bright was the life here; countless the baths; many a mead hall full of human mirth; these has Fate overturned; here men gazed on treasures, silver, gems; the baths were hot . . .'"

'It is very beautiful', said Alfred. 'Each phrase is like a gasp, a sob, a protest against mutability. It leads me on to think of your own emperor, Aurelius Ambrosianus, wearer of the bear-skin who men called Artos, "the bear" betrayed after his last battle at Camlan field; and of the Goddodin who fell bravely, at Catterick . . .'

"'*Diffugere nives!*"; Horace said it all long, long ago', Asser gently added, continuing to quote, "'The seasons return but when we go down to where father Aeneas

*67   Coin of King Alfred
struck at Ohsnaforda*

has gone, we are but dust" . . . but if you go to Bath you will see all has not been lost. There, in another of your cities, above the ruins where men and women still bathe in the hot and cold waters, is now a splendid church where Holy Virgins praise God in euphonious Latin chants. From Sulis Minerva to Our Lord and his Mother! I like to think that Togidubnus, who in his earthly life understood the many names of God, would have understood!'

'And so the Divine purpose goes on and on!' Alfred concurred, turning to Asser. 'History appears, at first glance, to sweep us on and away in a straight line, but in reality Time turns, just as the Seasons turn. We, too, renew ourselves as do the trees and the annual blooming of the roses. "Then God Himself overthrew death and put the devil to flight. He broke and overcame the doors of hell; the power of the devils was vanquished by the brightness of the light!"'

'Is that your own poem?' said Asser. Alfred smiled, as though in reply, but did not answer. Asser wished his Lord and King happy dreams and then retired to his own little room, for he had much work still to do. He lit a taper and carefully arranged a blank parchment, pens and ink on the table and began to write the long projected life of his friend and master, in the manner of Suetonius and of Einhard:

> 'To my most venerable and holy lord, Alfred, rector of all the Christians in the Island of Britain, king of the Angles and Saxons, Asser, lowest of all the servants of God, wishes a thousandfold prosperity in this life and the next, according to the desires of his prayers . . .'

68 *The church at Brixworth, Northamptonshire. The confident early Christian style, remi-niscent of the churches of Ravenna is a fitting symbol of 'Rome restored'. No doubt churches in Winchester and other parts of Wessex were similar*

The school at St Davids was still teaching the correct rhetorical Latin as that of the magister Eltutus, St Illtyd, at Llanilltud Fawr where St Samson of Dol had gone to school three centuries ago: 'lowest of all the servants of God . . .'. They had told him since he was a small child to begin a speech or a treatise like that. All the same, it was hard to feel quite so humble all the time. King Alfred had made him, a Briton, bishop of the great cathedral church at Sherborne and for his part he had helped the king to translate Boethius' masterpiece *The Consolation of Philosophy* into English.

His thoughts then turned to Italy where Boethius, the last of the great late Roman philosophers, had lived and died. Once those Romans came to what they thought was a savage island, beyond the Ocean, beyond the rim of the world. They arrived with a great army of four legions. Now we are returning the compliment as emissaries to the wide world, but with the honey of scholarship. The weapons of the Romans were swords and javelins; ours are books and pens. The tradition of correct Latin we fostered since the time of the Empire in Wales and the West, we in turn gave to those who called themselves Angles or Saxons. The combined learning of all the peoples of Britain had brought correct Latin back to the old continental provinces and even to Rome itself. It was true; even the Emperor Charlemagne with all his power had to beg Alcuin to come from York.

But our Alfred is a far better man and a truer Roman than Charles ever was. Charlemagne was a vigorous ruler, of course, but cruel . . . he could never be more than a Frankish barbarian. True greatness requires something more, much more! Asser took up his pen again: 'Alfred was born at the royal estate of Berkshire, named from Berroc Wood where the box-trees grow abundantly . . .' They called this kingdom the 'Kingdom of Wessex'; it had previously been the land of the Gewissae, who were in some ways the protectors of the old province of Britannia Prima, and before the province had been set up this had been the realm of the Great King, Togidubnus, friend of the Caesars. Had Togidubnus, too, enjoyed the aromatic perfume of box-trees in his palace garden near Chichester as his own king had done at Wantage?.

Ultima Cumaei venit iam carminis aetas;
magnus ab integro saeclorum nascitur ordo.

'We have reached the last age of the song of the Cumaean Sybil.
Time has given birth and the great Cycle of the Ages begins again.'

Asser quoted from Vergil's majestic Fourth Eclogue which he knew by heart, for did it not foretell the birth of Our Saviour? Then, recalling Boethius, he thought about Lady Philosophy. She had been born in Athens, the city named for Athene, goddess of Wisdom, and had come thence to Rome and her far-flung Empire. Here in Britain King Togidubnus had established welcoming homes for her, in the guise of Minerva, first in Chichester and then, even more splendidly, at Bath. She had been installed at Corinium and especially at Venta, our own Winchester where she still sits beside our King Alfred. She was at his cradle in Wantage, and is no doubt at work in other places in his realm as I write, at Dorchester certainly and at Sherborne; and what about Osnaforda? Certainly, there was a nice little nunnery there, established by a princess called Frideswide who is credited with miraculous powers and who, it is said, had come from a little circular Celtic-style convent at a place called Thornbury or Binsey, on the south side of the River Thames . . . but the idea of Lady Philosophy finding a home at Osnaforda was just too far-fetched. 'Osnaforda, indeed!'

Recalling himself to the theme of his meditation, he concluded that it was not the marching feet of Rome's legions which had made her great; her armies were no more. It was not the gold Rome had amassed now buried in the earth 'as useless to man as it was before'. There would be a heavy judgement to pay for those who indulged in gladiatorial displays and beast fights, but cruelty always removed one from the Truth. Asser picked up his pen again and applied it to the parchment, 'the pen and the book, these are our precious legacy from the Romans!'. He spoke these last words aloud, feeling all of a sudden relaxed, as though a great weight had been lifted from his soul. He was happy and now very optimistic about the future, despite the myriad cares which still beset his royal master and the realm of Wessex. The Dance of all the Years was, after all, now, as it had always been, in the guiding hands of the Most High God.

St Frideswide's day
Oxford, 19 October 2001

Glossary

alpha and omega   The first and last letters of the Greek alphabet, used by Christians to symbolise God (see Revelations 1.8 and 21.6)

architectus   An architect; in the army a military engineer

auloi   double pipes, often associated with satyrs

beneficiarius consularis   A legionary soldier seconded for policing duties such as looking after a mansio

cantharus   A two handled vessel used for serving wine, generally mixed with water. Frequent in both Bacchic and Christian contexts

chi-rho   The first two letters of the name of Christ, the first like a saltire cross and the second like a crook, the symbol both approximates to the Egyptian life symbol (ankh) and to the cross

civitas, civitates   The state or tribal area of a people, with an administrative capital (e.g. Corinium was the chief city of the Dobunni)

corona civica   A wreath of oak given for saving the lives of citizens in battle. From the reign of Augustus largely a prerogative of the emperors

domus   A house, in the sense of a grand town or country residence

Flavian dynasty   The family of Vespasian whose nomen was Flavius

grammaticus   Schoolteachers, teaching correct grammar and also literature, especially poetry

humanitas	The quality of being human in a good and noble sense; being civilized
mentula	A penis; often associated with the god Priapus renowned for his large erect phallus
nemet	Celtic for a sacred grove (the usual Latin name for a grove used in Italy was nemus)
neo-Platonism	The philosophy of Plato formalised into a religion especially from the third century. Neo-Platonists placed the Divine at the centre of all.
nundinum	A week of eight days culminating in a ninth, market day
paedeia	Education, culture (Greek)
sententia	An opinion, judgement, often in the form of a pithy phrase
signum, signa	A standard but also used for nick-names
syrinx	Pan pipes
thiasos	The companions of Bacchus (satyrs, maenads etc.). Neptune also had a thiasos (of tritons and nereids etc)
toga virilis	The plain white toga of manhood adopted by boys when they reached the age of about thirteen
topos, topoi	A stock category subject or description exemplified by Tacitean descriptions of battles or the means by which the Britons acquired humanitas. Education was often based around topoi. The word is, of course, Greek
tria nomina	The traditional Roman method of nomenclature consisting of a praenomen (e.g. Quintus), nomen (Natalius) and cognomen (Natalinus)

Further reading

The bibliographic origins of this book began with observations on the marble head of a child from Fishbourne, which I published in the *Journal of the British Archaeological Association* 149 (1996). Here I suggested that it was carved in Rome and showed Togidubnus at the time he assumed the *toga virilis* and was made a citizen by Claudius. This note was followed by a brief piece in *British Archaeology* 37 (1998) on 'Togidubnus and the British Liberation', and studies of the iconography of the Bath pediment in G.R. Tsetskhladze *et al.*, *Periplous. Papers presented to Sir John Boardman* (Thames and Hudson, London 2000) and in the *Oxford Journal of Archaeology* 18 (1999). There was also the paper that I wrote with Grahame Soffe on the sculpture in marble and bronze from Chichester and Bosham, published in the *Association for Roman Archaeology Bulletin* 8 (1999). In the autumn of 1999 and the early spring of 2000, I gave a lecture to the University of Glasgow and to the Society of Antiquaries of Scotland at both Edinburgh and Aberdeen on 'Roman Britain as Protectorate, Political Symbol and Military Training Ground', a resumé of which will appear in the *Proceedings of the Society of Antiquaries of Scotland*.

By the time I had produced these contributions, I found that much more had changed in my understanding of Roman Britain than simply accepting a new scenario for the invasion of AD 43 or 'discovering' one or two more clues towards reconstructing the outlines of the life of Britain's first 'Great King'. Almost everything I had previously read or thought about Roman Britain was now suspect or in need of drastic review. I included some of this radical rethinking in my part of *Roman Oxfordshire*, a book I wrote in concert with Paul Booth (see below), and was able to influence the 'storyline' of the admirable Roman display being laid out in the Oxfordshire Museum at Woodstock, but inevitably the 'full story' as I have come to see and feel it embraces more than just Oxfordshire. If I am right it affects the way the history of the entire province (or in late Roman terms, provinces) of Britannia should be understood in a fundamental manner. It was clearly vital for me to write a full-length book expounding my views.

A great many full-length studies and scholarly papers exist already dealing with most aspects of life in Roman Britain. The best general textbooks are still, in my opinion, Peter Salway, *Roman Britain* (Oxford History of England, 1981) and T.W. Potter and Catherine Johns, *Roman Britain* (BMP, London 1992). Guy de la Bédoyère's *Eagles over Britannia. The Roman Army in Britain* (Tempus 2001) surveys the Roman army and its achievements within the province, to which, of course, Guy accords a higher place than I do.

The classic 'conventional' account of the invasion and its aftermath is Graham Webster's *The Roman Invasion of Britain* (Batsford, London rev.edn 1993) together with *Rome against Caratacus* (Batsford, London rev. edn 1993) and *Boudica* (Batsford, London rev. edn 1993). If I have disagreed with Graham in my interpretation I hope I have been loyal to his belief that one has to be prepared to challenge any accepted theory, however 'professorial' the source. The difficulties inherent in the use of the sparse Classical sources have recently been highlighted, as far as the early period is concerned, by E.W. Black, 'The First Century Historians of Roman Britain', *OJA* 20 (2001), 415-28. Although I have interpreted the evidence for the most part differently, I agree that one cannot accept what one is told as fact just because the authority is Tacitus.

The text of this book was substantially complete by September 2001, which was when I first came upon Neil Faulkner's *The Decline and Fall of Roman Britain* (Tempus 2000) though I doubt that I would have changed anything even had I read it when it was first published. Indeed, it is clear that I present the opposite view to his, firmly believing that Roman civilization was in general a 'good thing' and that it neither declined nor fell, only changed, and that many Romans, far from being cheats or bullies, were conscientious and humane. Most of the 'Romans' one would have seen in Britain were, in any case, Britons with a scattering of Gauls amongst them. If my outlook is self-evidently 'élitist', that is because liberal culture always demands intellectual effort. But élite culture need not be limited nor exclusive and the aim of education ancient and modern has ever been to spread the gifts of learning. However, I do endorse Faulkner at one point where he writes (p11) 'The clash of competing "historical imaginations" is the way knowledge of the past advances.'

On Late Iron Age dynastic history I have drawn considerable inspiration from John Creighton, *Coins and Power in Late Iron Age Britain* (Cambridge 2000). John has certainly done a great deal to jolt received opinion. On Verica's realm taken strictly as the territory later ascribed to the Regni see Barry Cunliffe, *The Regni* (London 1973, and inevitably out of date) and his *Fishbourne Roman Palace* (revised edn, Tempus 1998) and Alec Down, *Roman Chichester* (Phillimore, Chichester 1988) are useful. On the likely West Sussex focus of the invasion see D. Bird, 'The Claudian invasion campaign reconsidered', *OJA* 19 (2000), 91-104. The Fishbourne palace is placed in its local context by David Rudling in 'The development of Roman villas in Sussex', *Sussex Archaeological Collections* 136 (1998), 41-65, though it is a pity that he did not include a few of the early villas in the nearer part of Hampshire. For the Catuarus ring see Roger Tomlin, 'Reading a 1st-century Roman signet ring from Fishbourne', *SAC* 135 (1997), 127-30. Finally, another most important recent paper in the same journal (John Manley, 'Measurement and metaphor: the design and meaning of building 3 at Fishbourne Roman Palace', *SAC* 138 (2000), 103-13), suggests that the symmetry of one of the ancillary buildings of the palace, laid out in accordance with Vitruvian precepts, might imply that it had a metaphorical significance.

The classic work on Silchester remains George Boon's *Silchester. The Roman town of Calleva* (David and Charles, Newton Abbot 1974) which has largely withstood the test of time despite the important recent excavations by Mike Fulford, which have elucidated something of the *oppidum* underneath, at least insofar as cultural life is concerned. To these should be added various other works dealing with southern Britain in the Roman period including Barry Cunliffe, *Roman Bath Discovered* (4th edn Tempus 2000); Peter Ellis (ed.), *Roman Wiltshire and After* (Wiltshire Heritage 2001); M. Henig and P. Booth, *Roman Oxfordshire* (Sutton Publishing, Stroud 2000) and Rosalind Niblett, *Verulamium*.

The Roman City of St Albans (Tempus 2001). A paper that I wrote with Grahame Soffe (M. Henig and G. Soffe, 'The Thruxton Roman villa and its mosaic pavement', *JBAA* 146 (1993), 1–28) deals both with the artistic and religious aspects of the mosaic, but more crucially here, Grahame Soffe's work in putting these Hampshire villas into their proper context helps us to appreciate how British farmers became 'Roman'. Barry Cunliffe's Danebury Environs project is continuing to explore this theme.

On the flourishing artistic life of Britannia see my own *The Art of Roman Britain* (Batsford, London 1995), though I now believe that the army played a very much less important rôle in disseminating ideas. Behind that book, of course, lies J.M.C. Toynbee's magisterial *Art in Britain under the Romans* (Oxford 1964), an enormous quarry of material. It is, however, more than a mere catalogue and can be read for its judgements, which are often profound. Barry Cunliffe's and Michael Fulford's fascicule of the *Corpus Signorum Imperii Romani* (British Academy 1982) dealing with the sculpture from much of the region likewise deserves commendation, not least for its title 'Bath and the Rest of Wessex' which for fifteen years I thought anachronistic, but I now see as yet another example of Barry's insight into the region. As this book proclaims in no uncertain terms I, too, now think of this part of Roman Britain as 'Wessex', though I have taken the liberty of adding Gloucestershire and West Oxfordshire, the lands of the allied Dobunni, which in the post-Roman period became associated with the Hwicce of Wychwood and were thus associated with Mercia. The sculpture from these counties was the subject of my own fascicule of *CSIR*, 'Roman Sculpture from the Cotswold Region' (British Academy) which was published in 1993. With regard to architecture, the general reader could do no better than consult Guy de la Bédoyère's *The Buildings of Roman Britain* (Tempus 2001).

My survey of *Religion in Roman Britain* (Batsford, London 1984) suffers rather more from a Roman official bias than my book on art. When I wrote it I was forever looking towards influence from on top and from outside, and I am glad that my late friend, Graham Webster, who encouraged me and inspired me so often, provided such a useful corrective in *The British Celts and their Gods under Rome* (Batsford 1986). As in several places I have brought out the importance of sexual symbolism in ancient beliefs it seems appropriate to cite Catherine Johns' *Sex or Symbol. Erotic Images of Greece and Rome* (BMP, London 1982), which is inspirational like everything she writes. Another work by Catherine Johns and Timothy Potter, *The Thetford Treasure. Roman Jewellery and Silver* (BMP, London 1983) is essential for the understanding of late Roman pagan cults. To this should be added Bryn Walters' illuminating paper 'The "Orpheus" mosaic in Littlecote Park, England', in R. Farioli Campanati, *III colloquio internazionale sul mosaico antico* (Ravenna 1984), 433–42. Charles Thomas, *Christianity in Roman Britain to AD 500* (Batsford 1981) is the standard work on the Christian church in Britain though it should now be used in conjunction with C.F. Mawer, *Evidence for Christianity in Roman Britain. The small-finds* (BAR British series 243, Oxford 1995).

For inscriptions, R.G. Collingwood and R.P. Wright, *The Roman Inscriptions of Britain* (*RIB*) of which volume I first appeared in 1965 is an essential aid. Literary texts and a selection of inscriptions in translation are conveniently assembled in S. Ireland, *Roman Britain. A sourcebook* (2nd edn Routledge 1996).

I have been stimulated by John Onians' thoughts about Antiquity since we were students together at Cambridge; he has influenced me much more than any other historian of Classical art and, for me, his *Classical Art and the Cultures of Greece and Rome* (Yale University Press, New Haven and London, 1999) is by far the best introduction to the manner in which the Romans thought about themselves and brought their rhetorical training and imagination to bear on a distinctive outlook on the world which, nevertheless, changed over time. Onians' book certainly contains a great deal which explains what Togidubnus' intellectual baggage as a highly educated Roman citizen must have included. To see the king in his north-west European context, however, one has also to read Greg Woolf, *Becoming Roman. The origins of provincial civilization in Gaul* (Cambridge 1998) which is another one of those studies which shakes the foundations of what we once thought we knew; certainly Romano-British studies have not yet fully come to terms with it.

The reigns of Carausius and Allectus form the prelude to the remarkable story of fourth-century Britain and P.J. Casey, *Carausius and Allectus. The British Usurpers* (Batsford 1994) is an elegant account of their reigns. Guy de la Bédoyère made the brilliant discovery that certain runs of letters on coins of Carausius alluded to Vergil's fourth *Eclogue* ('Carausius and the marks RSR and I.N.P.C.D.A.', *Num. Chron.* 158 (1998), 79-88. The culture of fourth century Britain is admirably surveyed by Guy de la Bédoyère, *The Golden Age of Roman Britain* (Tempus 1999) and by Sarah Scott, *Art and Society in Fourth-Century Britain. Villa Mosaics in Context* (Oxford University School of Archaeology monograph no. 53, 2000). As I have endowed the Stonesfield mosaic with rather a key role in this book, it is worth mentioning the recent paper by Tom Freshwater, Jill Draper, Sarah Hinds and myself, 'From Stone to Textile: The Bacchus Mosaic at Stonesfield, Oxon, and the Stonesfield Embroidery', *JBAA* 153 (2000), 1-29.

What happened after the fourth century is the theme of Ken Dark, *Civitas to Kingdom. British Political Continuity 300-800* (Leicester University Press 1994), the same author's *Britain and the End of the Roman Empire* (Tempus 2000), Ellen Swift, *The End of the Western Roman Empire. An Archaeological Investigation* (Tempus 2000), and of Charles Thomas, *Christian Celts. Messages and Images* (Tempus 1998). Behind them all is John Morris's classic *The Age of Arthur* (Weidenfeld and Nicolson 1973), an inspiration even where he is wrong. I am especially grateful to Charles for leading me to make one or two discoveries about the nature of literacy in Roman Britain. With regard to literary texts this is explored in a number of books by D.R. Howlett notably *The Celtic Latin Tradition of Biblical Style* (Four Courts Press, Dublin 1995). John Cowper Powys's *Porius* (Macdonald, London 1951) is a wonderfully imaginative evocation of what it felt like to live in western Britain at the end of the fifth century, between Rome and the early Middle Ages. The writings of St Patrick and Gildas alone show that something essential of Roman Britain was alive and flourishing long after the purported date of its decease; they are conveniently available in two volumes of *History from the Sources* (Phillimore, London and Chichester 1978). On the fundamental cultural changes brought about by the spread of Christianity in Late Antiquity all the books of Peter Brown are of the highest interest including *The World of Late Antiquity* (Thames and Hudson 1971) and *The Cult of the Saints* (SCM Press 1981).

The 'Anglo-Saxon' period is a very large subject on which I venture with considerable trepidation, simply in order to follow a few continuing 'Roman' threads. On a European scale this has been done rather well in L. Webster and M. Brown, *The Transformation of the Roman World AD 400-900* (BMP, London 1997). For St Albans see M. Henig and P. Lindley, *Alban and St Albans. Roman and Medieval Architecture, Art and Archaeology* (BAA Conference Transactions 24, 2001). L. Webster and J. Backhouse, *The Making of England. Anglo-Saxon Art and Culture AD 600-900* (BMP 1991) contains a great deal of fascinating material from the time of the conversion. Oxfordshire, where I live, has long had a particular fascination for me and John Blair's *Anglo-Saxon Oxfordshire* (Sutton Publishing, Stroud 1994) is packed with insights. Eric Fernie, *The Architecture of the Anglo-Saxons* (Batsford 1983) is a starting place for early Church building. On 'The Ruin' and Bath see Barry Cunliffe, 'Earth's Grip Holds Them', in B. Hartley and J. Wacher, *Rome and the Northern Provinces. Papers presented to Sheppard Frere* (Trowbridge 1983), 67-83. David Sturdy in *Alfred the Great* (Constable, London 1995), is enthusiastic in his advocacy, and passionate (as in everything he writes), encouraging the reader to find out still more about the fascinating life and times of the king. Asser's sensitive contemporary life of King Alfred is printed in translation in S. Keynes and M. Lapidge, *Alfred the Great* (Penguin Books, Harmondsworth 1983). For a very different kind of book but which takes the 'inheritance' from this point on to the end of the Middle Ages see D.A. Hinton, *Alfred's Kingdom. Wessex and the South 800-1500* (J.M. Dent, London 1977).

Texts of Vergil and Ovid as well as most other ancient writers can be found in the Loeb Classical Library together with English translations. Vergil's *Eclogues* including the Fourth Eclogue central to this book were included with the Latin text and a translation by E.V. Rieu in Vergil, *The Pastoral Poems* (Harmondsworth 1954).The great fourth-century poem the *Pervigilium Veneris* which I have placed at the heart of a crucial chapter, as an accompaniment to a dance by three boys and a girl, a transmutation of Poussin's glorious vision, will be found in its entirety in F. Brittain (ed.), *The Penguin Book of Latin Verse* (Harmondsworth 1962), 72-9. The best book I have ever read on the power of the old gods and of neo-platonic thought, albeit in a Greek ambience, is Polymnia Athanassiadi, *Julian. An intellectual biography* (London 1992). The Emperor Julian as it happens had a major influence on events in fourth-century Gaul and Britain; what he thought was important and the story of his intellectual development cannot be without relevance to the cultured gentry of Britain who in many instances would have been well versed in Greek literature.

Taking my theme beyond what many readers will consider 'real' archaeology, but nevertheless into territory very much germane to the moral and religious outlook of this book, is Edgar Wind's *Pagan Mysteries in the Renaissance* (London 1958). On the painting, which helped to inspire my treatment of the theme, the Wallace Collection has published an admirable monograph by Richard Beresford entitled *A Dance to the Music of Time by Nicolas Poussin* (London 1995). On Claude see Humphrey Wine, *Claude. The Poetic Landscape* (National Gallery, London 1994).

Index